Intellectual Property Law in China

Intellectual Property Law in China

Second Edition

Hong Xue

This book was originally published as a monograph in the International Encyclopaedia of Laws/Intellectual Property Law.

General Editors: Roger Blanpain, Frank Hendrickx
Volume Editor: Hendrik Vanhees

Wolters Kluwer

Published by:
Kluwer Law International
PO Box 316
2400 AH Alphen aan den Rijn
The Netherlands
Website: www.wklawbusiness.com

Sold and distributed in North, Central and South America by:
Aspen Publishers, Inc.
7201 McKinney Circle
Frederick, MD 21704
United States of America
Email: customer.service@aspenpublishers.com

Sold and distributed in all other countries by:
Turpin Distribution Services Ltd.
Stratton Business Park
Pegasus Drive, Biggleswade
Bedfordshire SG18 8TQ
United Kingdom
Email: kluwerlaw@turpin-distribution.com

ISBN 978-90-411-6247-2

This title is available on www.kluwerlawonline.com

The Author

Dr Hong Xue is a Professor of Law and Director of the Institute for the Internet Policy & Law at Beijing Normal University (BNU). Before joining BNU, she was an associate professor with the Faculty of Law, University of Hong Kong. Prof. Xue specializes in intellectual property law, information technology law, and Internet governance. Prof. Xue is a fellow of the Yale Information Society Project. Prof. Xue was elected as one of the Ten Nationally Distinguished Young Jurists by the China Law Society. She works in many governmental and non-governmental organizations. She is on the Advisory Committee of the United Nations Network of Experts for Paperless Trade in Asia and the Pacific (UNNExT). She is an arbitrator at China International Economic and Trade Arbitration Commission (CIETAC), Nanjing International Arbitration Institute, Shenzhen Arbitration Commission, as well as a UDRP neutral at World Intellectual Property Organization (WIPO) and Asia Domain Names Dispute Resolution Center (ADNDRC). She is the Chair of Council of Chinese Domain Name Users Alliance and the Faculty Chair of Asia Pacific Internet Leadership Project (APILP) in Beijing. She is in the Editorial Board of World Intellectual Property Journal and the Expert Advisory Board of Diplo Foundation. She is one of the founders of the Internet Users Organization in the Asia-Pacific Region.

The Author

Table of Contents

Table of Contents

List of Abbreviations

Glossary

General Principles	General Principles of Civil Law of the People's Republic of China
CNY	Chinese Yuan Renmibi
Internet Regulations	Regulations for Protection of the Right of Communication via the Information Network
IPR	Intellectual Property Right
NPC	National People's Congress
PRC	People's Republic of China
SIPO	State Intellectual Property Office
Software Regulations	Regulations on the Protection of Computer Software
WTO	World Trade Organization

List of Abbreviations

General Introduction

§1. General Background

I. Geography

1. China is the third-largest country in the world, behind Russia and Canada. China is a very diverse land including deserts, mountains, and fertile river basins. Much of western China is mountainous with the Himalaya, Tian, and Pamir ranges. Western China also has a large desert. Central China consists of mountainous regions. Rivers also play a major role in China, both for transportation and for irrigation. Much of the northern wheat fields and southern rice fields are irrigated from rivers.

II. Cultural Composition

2. China has a civilian history of more than 5,000 years full of artistic, philosophical, political, and scientific advancement. Though regional differences provide a sense of diversity, commonalities in language and religion connect a culture distinguished by such contributions as Confucianism and Taoism. Confucianism was the official philosophy throughout most of Imperial China's history, and traditional Chinese culture is heavily influenced by it.

3. With the rise of Western economic and military power over China beginning in the mid-nineteenth century, however, non-Chinese systems of social and political organization gained adherents in China. Since then, China has been in the conflicts of the strengths of Chinese and Western cultures. In essence, the history of twentieth-century China is one of experimentation to find a new system of social, political, and economic organization that would allow for the reintegration of the nation in the wake of dynastic collapse.

III. Political System

4. The Constitution is the fundamental law of China. The existing Constitution was adopted for implementation by the Fifth Session of the Fifth National People's Congress on December 1982. Amendments were made to the Constitution, respectively, at the First Session of the Seventh National People's Congress on April 1988, the First Session of the Eighth National People's Congress on 29 March 1993, and the Second Session of the Ninth National People's Congress on 15 March 1999.

5. The People's Republic of China was founded by the Communist Party of China, which is the ruling political party of the Chinese people.

6. The socialist system led by the working class and based on the alliance of the workers and farmers is the fundamental system of the People's Republic of China.

7. The National People's Congress, with the Standing Committee, is the highest organ of State power and the highest legislature of the country. Local people's congresses are local organs of State power. The Supreme People's Court is the highest judiciary of China. The Chinese judicial hierarchical system has four levels of the courts (so-called 'people's courts'), i.e. the Supreme People's Court, High People's Courts, Intermediate People's Courts and Basic People's Courts.

IV. Population Statistics

8. The population of China is more than 1.3 billion people. This is about one-fifth of the world's population.

§2. Historical Background

9. The Chinese contemporary legal system for the protection of intellectual property has been developing with the economic reform and the foreign trade. China's intellectual property system was largely established during the 1980s and revised for the accession to the World Trade Organization (WTO) during the 1990s. On December 2001, China finally became a member of the WTO, and Chinese intellectual property laws entered into post-WTO times. China gradually becomes the world's second largest economy in the first fifteen years of the twenty-first Century, and Chinese intellectual property system undergoes significant developments to meet the changing social economic situation.

10. The State Council approved the Guidelines for the National Strategy of Intellectual Property, which was prepared by the State Intellectual Property Office and other relevant government departments in April 2008. The National Strategy exerts positive influence on perfecting China's system of intellectual property, promoting creativity and innovation in the Chinese people and economy, and supporting the exploitation of resulting intellectual property.

§3. Specialized Intellectual Property Courts

11. In November 2013, Communist Party of China (CPC), the ruling Party of China, released the roadmap for China's further social economic reform and development at the Third Plenary Session of the 18th CPC Central Committee. In that landmark policy document, CPC committed to strengthen protection of intellectual property rights, improve the mechanism to encourage innovation, and explore ways of setting up the specialized IP courts. In line with the roadmap, the State Council, the highest administration of China, published the '2014–2020 Action Plan for the Thorough Implementation of the National Intellectual Property Strategy' on 10 December 2014, which aims to significantly improve the capacity to create, use, protect and manage intellectual property rights.

For the purpose of deepening and furthering the judicial reforms, the Chinese National People's Congress Standing Committee made the 'Decision to Establish the Specialized Intellectual Property (IP) Courts in Beijing, Shanghai and Guangzhou' on 31 August 2014. Accordingly, China's first specialized intellectual property court was officially unveiled in Beijing on 6 November 2014. The other two specialized IP courts were established later in Shanghai and Guangzhou respectively before the end of 2014. These specialized IP courts have accepted their first batch of cases. The Supreme People's Court issued on 31 October 2014 the 'Stipulations on the Scope and Jurisdiction of the Specialized Intellectual Property Courts in Beijing, Shanghai and Guangzhou' (SPC Stipulations), which entered into effect on 3 November 2014.

According to the SPC's Stipulations, the specialized IP courts are responsible for the following types of cases:

(a) all first instance civil or administrative cases involving invention, utility and design patents, plant variety protection rights, layout designs of integrated circuits, ownership of technical secrets and copyrights for computer software;
(b) appeal cases against administrative decisions made by the departments of the State Council and local governments above county level involving copyright, trademarks and unfair competition; and,
(c) all civil cases where the recognition of a well-known trademark is involved.

As far as a case is among the specified types, it falls into the specialized IP courts' judicial power irrespective of whether it contains the other unspecified elements. For example, a trademark infringement civil dispute in which the recognition of a well-known trademark is involved shall be tried by the specialized IP court. Under the SPC Stipulations, the specialized IP courts' judicial power only extend to the listed types of civil cases, rather than all civil cases involving IP disputes. With respect to the unspecified civil cases, such as copyright ownership or infringement disputes involving copyright works other than computer software, their first instance jurisdiction should still be determined according to the general rules of Chinese Civil Procedure Law.

Chapter 1. Copyright and Neighbouring Rights

§1. Sources: Legislation

12. China is a civil law country. The General Principles of Civil Law of the People's Republic of China (General Principles), which were adopted on 12 April 1986 and went into effect 1 January 1987, are the basic civil laws. A Civil Code is now being drafted by the State legislature – the Chinese National People's Congress.

13. Article 94 of the General Principles provides that citizens and entities enjoying copyright are entitled to control making their works public, to have authorship attributed for creating works, and to obtain remuneration for the use of works. Article 118 assures citizens and entities of relief against the infringement of copyrights, of trademarks and of patents, as well as of other rights in products of mind. This provision further specifies that such relief should include orders to cease infringement, to eliminate its effects, and to compensate for any resulting losses. The General Principles also set out general rules concerning torts and contracts in civil cases that may have diverse relations to copyright. The Tort Liability Law of the People's Republic of China, adopted on 26 December 2009, effective 1 July 2010, sets out detailed rules concerning tort liability and legal remedies. Copyright is one of the private rights that the Tort Liability Law protects.

14. More than forty years after it was founded, China enacted the first Copyright Law on 7 September 1990, which went into effect 1 June 1991. On 27 October 2001, the Standing Committee of the Chinese National People's Congress adopted and promulgated the Decision on Revision of the Copyright Law of the People's Republic of China ('2001 revision'). This decision brought into effect the first revision of the Chinese Copyright Law since its enactment in 1990. Indeed, only forty-five days before China became a member of the WTO, this revision made Chinese Copyright Law more consistent with the TRIPs Agreement. On 26 February 2010, the Standing Committee of the Chinese National People's Congress adopted and promulgated the Decision on Revision of the Copyright Law of the People's Republic of China ('2010 revision'), effective 1 April 2010. Although the 2010 revision is the second revision to the Copyright Law, it merely affects two provisions, namely Articles 4 and 26, respectively, and keeps the rest of the 2001 revision intact.

On 31 March 2012, the National Copyright Administration released a First Draft of a proposed third revision of the Copyright Law for public consultation. The Draft immediately attracted public and media attention, while musicians, collecting societies, the Internet industry, and many other stakeholder groups opposed many provisions in this initial draft. On 6 July 2012, the National Copyright Administration released a Second Draft, in which eighty-one provisions were changed from the first one. On 6 June 2014, the National Copyright Administration released the Official Draft to be submitted to the State Council for review. The Official Draft, which is actually the Third Draft, was open for public comments and consultation until 5 July 2014. The Third Draft, after being reviewed by the State Council, is supposed to be submitted to the Standing Committee of the National People's Congress. The pending third revision aims to integrate sporadic sources of copyright law and set out a comprehensive and coherent legal system of copyright. The Third Draft is still subject to lively debate and, eventually, further proposals for change. There has been no timetable set out for completion of the third revision of the Copyright Law. 14: The Copyright Law authorized the State Council to issue regulations in the field of copyright. Pursuant to that mandate, the following regulations have been issued:

(a) Implementing regulations: On 2 August 2002, the State Council promulgated the Regulations on Implementing the Copyright Law. These Implementing Regulations entered into force on 15 September 2002. The State Council made the Decision on the Revision of the Regulations on 16 January 2013, effective from 1 March 2013, to strengthen administrative sanctions against copyright infringements.
(b) Software Regulations: On 20 December 2001, the State Council promulgated the Regulations on the Protection of Computer Software. These Software Regulations went into effect 1 January 2002, superseding the prior Software Regulations that had been promulgated on 4 June 1991. On 20 February 2002, the National Copyright Administration of China enacted the Rules of the Registration of Computer Software Copyright, under which the China Copyright Protection Centre was accredited as the software registration organ. On 30 January 2013, the State Council promulgated the Decision on the Revision of the Regulations, effective from 1 March 2013, which modifies one provision to strengthen administrative enforcement for software copyright.
(c) Internet Regulations: On 18 May 2006, the State Council enacted the 'Regulations for Protection of the Right of Communication via the Information Network'. These Regulations were enacted according to Article 58 of the Copyright Law and went into effect 1 July 2006.
(d) Collective management: On 28 December 2004, the State Council promulgated the Regulations on the Collective Management of Copyright. These Regulations went into effect 1 March 2005.

15. Chinese courts, like others following the civil law, are not bound by precedents such as would apply according to the principle of *stare decisis*. Chinese case law rather illustrates judicial practice, in which the courts may consider, *inter alia*, the legislative record, persuasive decisions by other courts, and internal judicial documents.

16. The most important of these internal judicial documents are the guidelines that China's Supreme People's Court lays out for the lower courts to help them interpret various laws, including copyright laws. For example, the Supreme Court has issued the Interpretation of Several Issues Relating to the Application of Law to the Civil Dispute Cases regarding Damaging the Right of Communication via Information Network, adopted at the 1561st session of the Judicial Committee of the Supreme People's Court on 26 November 2012, effective on 1 January 2013 and the other guidelines to help with the matters such as conducting copyright trials; resolving disputes concerning unfair competition; resolving conflicts between copyright, trademarks, and other such rights; and, jointly with the Supreme People's Attorney General, handling crimes against intellectual property rights. The lower courts may also request the Supreme People's Court for authoritative interpretations with regard to specific issues of law, and all lower courts may then consult the Supreme People's Court's replies that are published in its Gazettes. For example, on 13 October 2005, the Supreme People's Court and the Supreme People's Attorney General jointly published a reply with respect to handling criminal cases of copyright infringement involving sound or video recordings.

In addition to the guidelines on practical matters, the Supreme People's Court also publishes a series of intellectual property policy documents, which, although not capable of being applied directly in judicial decisions, serve to ensure the lower courts' exercise of discretional power consistent with the national intellectual property strategy. Since November 2010, the Supreme People's Court, in accordance with the Stipulations regarding the Work of Guiding Cases, has published a series of Guiding Cases, including intellectual property cases, for the reference of all lower courts, irrespective of their location or judicial level.

§2. Protected Subject Matter

I. Different Categories of Protected Works

17. The Copyright Law protects works with copyright and grants neighbouring rights in performances, sound and video recordings, radio and television broadcasts, and typographical formats.

18. Article 3 of the Copyright Law defines the 'works' that the Law protects as including 'works of literature, art, natural science, social science, engineering technology' and the like, which are expressed in the listed nine categories. The list is not exhaustive and a type of work not expressly included in the list will be protected if further law identifies it. For example, the Copyright Law authorizes the State Council to draw up regulations on the protection of folklore, and the case law has protected folklore even though no regulations have yet been issued on point.

19. The Implementing Regulations give short definitions of the nine categories that Article 3 of the Copyright Law sets out. These definitions may be set down as follows:

(a) 'Written' or 'literary works' are those expressed in writing, such as novels, poems, essays, theses, and other such works.
(b) 'Oral works' are those that are orally expressed and have not been fixed in any material form, for example, unprepared speeches, lectures, and debates.
(c) 'Musical, dramatic, *quyi*, choreographic, and acrobatic works' may all be performed. Musical works include works with or without accompanying words, for example, songs or symphonies. Dramatic works, such as plays, operas, and local

forms, are created for live performance, notably, on stage. *Quyi* works are based on traditional forms created mainly for performance through recitation, music, or both, and include storytelling, ballad singing, comic dialogs, clapper talks, and cross talks. Choreographic works are expressed in successive body or facial movements, gestures, or mime. Acrobatic works are expressed through body movements, for example, in circus acts.

(d) 'Works of fine art and architectural works' constitute another category. Works of fine art are two- or three-dimensional objects created in lines, colours, etc. When viewed, works of painting, calligraphy, and sculpture, for example, impart aesthetic effect. Architectural works, being expressly added to this category, are the works expressed in the form of buildings or other architectural structures that, when viewed, impart aesthetic effect.
(e) 'Photographic works', after the 2001 revision, became an independent category, referring to works created by recording images on light-sensitive materials with the aid of devices.
(f) 'Cinematographic works' include 'works expressed by a process analogous to cinematography'. They may be recorded on some material support, are made up of a series of images with or without accompanying sound, and are capable of being projected with the aid of suitable devices or communicated to the public in other ways. If a cinematographic work is merely recorded onto a video tape, the resulting audiovisual recording is only a copy rather than an independent work, due to the lack of originality.
(g) 'Drawings of engineering designs and product designs, illustrations, maps, and models' often portray or describe objects that can actually be constructed or manufactured.
(h) 'Computer software', under Article 2 of the Software Regulations, is defined as computer programs and related documentation.

II. Works Excluded from Protection

20. Under Article 5 of the Copyright Law, the following items are not subject to copyright protection:

(a) laws, regulations, resolutions, decisions, and orders of State organs; other documents of a legislative, administrative, or judicial nature; and official translations of all such works;
(b) news on current affairs; or
(c) calendars, numerical tables, or forms of general use and formulas.

21. Article 4 of the Copyright Law was revised in 2010 revision, i.e., a work is no longer excluded from copyright protection even if the State may supervise and administer the publication and circulation of the work under the Constitution according to law or in the public interest.

III. Special Categories of Works

A. Computer Software

22. The Copyright Law enumerates software among the types of works it protects, while the Software Regulations implement such protection.

23. In the Chinese Copyright Law, the term 'software' includes, in addition to the program code, related 'documentation': It thus refers to written materials and diagrams, for example, and user manuals, flow charts, etc., that use natural or formalized language to describe the contents, composition, design, functions, specifications, development, testing results, and methods of use of the program code. The term 'computer program' includes both source and object codes. 'Source code' refers to a series of symbolically expressed instructions or sentences that can be automatically converted into a series of coded instructions, and 'object code' refers to such coded instructions that can be executed on information-processing equipment such as computers in order to obtain a certain result.

24. The Software Regulations further specify the Chinese regime for protecting computer programs. To be protected, software must be developed independently and must be fixed in a tangible medium of expression.

B. Databases

25. The Copyright Law does not include express provision on databases. However, a database that is qualified as a compilation work is copyrightable.

26. After the 2001 revision, works created by compiling a number of works, parts of works, or unprotected data or other materials are protected as compilation works, provided that the selection or arrangement of their contents constitutes an intellectual creation. The copyright in a work created by compilation is enjoyed by the compiler who, in cases of large-scale compilations, is often an entity. The relevant provision also precludes the exercise of such copyright from prejudicing copyright in the prior works included in the compilation.

C. Other

27. Derivative works are works based on a prior work or works, such as the adaptation of a novel into a film or a translation from English to Chinese. Article 5 of the Implementing Regulations defines processes by which derivative works are created.

28. 'Adaptation' is the creation of new works on the basis of pre-existing ones by changing their original form of expression or the purpose that they were originally designed to serve. 'Translation' is the process of converting the language of a work into another language, while an 'annotation' is an explanation of terms used in works, such as symbols, Chinese or other writing characters, words or sentences, etc. 'Arrangement' is the process of changing the fragmented or otherwise poorly ordered materials of a prior work or prior works or materials into a more systematic and orderly form.

29. Under Article 12 of the Copyright Law, where a work is created by adaptation, translation, annotation, or arrangement, the author creating that derivative work enjoys a separate copyright in it, but may not exercise that copyright to prejudice the copyright in any prior, underlying work. For example, an annotator or arranger will thus enjoy copyright only to the extent of his annotation or arrangement, but not in the materials annotated or arranged, and he or she will not be entitled to prohibit third parties from annotating or arranging these underlying materials.

§3. Conditions of Protection

I. Formal Requirements

30. The Copyright Law protects a work as soon as it is created by its author. A work is understood to be 'created' not only when the whole work is created, but also if only a part of the work is created so long as that part is a complete expression of the author's idea in a certain form, such as a part of a novel published in a newspaper.

31. Fixation in a tangible or durable form is generally not required. Of course, many types of works – such as maps, sketches, cinematographic works, and drawings of engineering and product designs – are 'by nature' fixed in a tangible form upon creation, but this is not a 'legal' requirement. Chinese Copyright Law also protects oral works that may be created without fixation and that, in many cases, are not embodied in a tangible means of expression.

32. Nonetheless, according to Article 2 of the Implementing Regulations, works are only protected by copyright if they are capable of reproduction in a tangible form. For example, under Article 2 of the Supreme People's Court's guidelines on online liability, works in digital form, whether or not of a type listed in Article 3 of the Copyright Law, are protected if they are susceptible of reproduction in a tangible form.

II. Substantive Requirements

33. The term 'works', as used in Chinese copyright law, refers to 'creations' in the literary, artistic, and scientific domains. The key to the meaning of the term 'creations', in turn, lies in the requirement of originality.

34. Authors must originate works by their own intellectual activities. A mere copier cannot therefore become the author of a work. Furthermore, neither arranging for others to create works nor providing them with consultation, material resources, and supporting services for their creative activities may be deemed creative acts.

35. Furthermore, a routine change in a prior work does not constitute intellectual creation. For example, after the claimant in a case submitted a calligraphic work consisting of four Chinese characters *Tian Xia Liang Cang* (the National Grains Storehouse) and a few ink marks (dots, lines, strips, etc.) scattered among the characters, the commissioning parties used the four characters *Tian Xia Liang Cang* as the title of a television play but deleted the ink marks. The court found that deleting these marks did not generate any further matter protected by copyright.[1]

36. To be protected, a work need not display marked 'creativity' or 'novelty'. More generally, there is no requirement that the work must have some merit, above and beyond originating in an author's intellectual activities. Furthermore, under generally recognized principles of copyright doctrine, copyright protection extends to expressions but not to ideas, procedures, methods of operation, or mathematical concepts as such.

§4. Ownership

I. The Author (Original Authorship)

37. Article 11 of the Copyright Law confirms that, except in cases subject to specific provisions of law to the contrary, the copyright in a work initially belongs to the author who created the work. It provides that, until proved to the contrary, the citizen or entity whose name is mentioned in connection with a work will be presumed to be the author of the work. The proof may be the manuscripts, original copy, legitimate publications, certificates of copyright registration or statements made by the certifying organization.[2]

38. Under Article 11 of the Law, the author of a work is the citizen who has created the work. Where a work is created according to the intention and under the supervision and responsibility of a legal entity or other organization, such legal entity or organization shall be deemed to be the author of the work. Copyright enjoyed by the State is to be enforced by the National Copyright Administration on behalf of the State.[3]

---

1. *Du Benji v. Writer's Press*, Beijing Chaoyang District People's Court, 20 Oct. 2003, overruled partially, Beijing Second Intermediate People's Court, 16 Dec. 2003.
2. Interpretation of several issues relating to the adjudication of, and the application of Copyright Law to, cases of civil disputes on copyright, adopted at the 1,246th session of the Judicial Committee of the Supreme People's Court on 12 Oct. 2002, effective on 15 Oct. 2002.
3. Implementing Regulations, Art. 16.

II. Joint Works/Works Created by Several Persons

39. Under Article 13 of the Copyright Law, when two or more authors create a work jointly, they will enjoy copyright in the work jointly. Article 13 further makes clear that anyone who has not participated in the creation of the work – for example, one who only provided a financial, administrative, or technical contribution – may not be treated as a co-author. The different authors of concurrent works may independently enjoy the copyright in their individual works, provided that the works were created independently and have originality.

40. Article 13 concludes by providing that, if a work of joint authorship can be separated into independent parts and if these can be exploited separately, each co-author is entitled to an independent copyright in each part that he or she has created but may not exercise such copyright to prejudice the copyright in the joint work as a whole. Under Article 9 of the Implementing Regulations, if the parts of a work of joint authorship cannot be used separately and if the joint authors fail to reach an agreement on the exercise of copyright in the entire work, no party may unreasonably prohibit the exercise of that copyright, except for the right of assignment in the whole work, and all the income deriving from the exploitation of the work shall be fairly allocated to all the co-authors.

III. Works Made for Hire

41. Where an entity requests, supervises, and is responsible for the creation of a work, it will be deemed to be the author of the work.

42. Chinese law uses the term 'occupational work' or 'work created in the course of employment' in Article 16 of the Copyright Law. In the following two cases, the author of the occupational work enjoys the moral right to credit for authorship, while the employing entity enjoys all other rights, both moral and economic, and is to reward the author for creating the work:

(a) works including, but not limited to, drawings and descriptions of engineering and product designs, computer software, and maps that are created in the course of employment under the responsibility of the employing entity and with material resources, notably equipment or materials, which that entity expressly provided for such creation; and
(b) works that are created in the course of employment where the copyright is, in accordance with laws, administrative regulations, or contracts, enjoyed by the employing entity.

43. Except for the circumstances set out in the final paragraph of Article 16, when a citizen creates a work in the fulfilment of a task assigned to him or her by the employing entity, he or she enjoys the copyright in this occupational work, but the entity may exploit the work within the scope of its professional or business activities. Further, for two years after the completion of the work, the author may not, without the consent of the employing entity, authorize a third party to exploit the work in the same way as the entity may exploit it. Thus, the employing entity has, by law, a license to use the work in its professional or business activities, and this license is exclusive for two years subject to the conditions. This two-year term starts running on the date on which the author delivers the work to the employing entity. Where, however, the entity does not use the work in the course of its business within these two years, the author may request it to permit a third party to use the work in the same manner as it would have been entitled to, and it may not refuse such a request without proper cause. In such a situation, during these two years, the author and the employing entity are to share, according to proportions on which they agree, any resulting remuneration from the third-party use of the work.

44. However, copyright in software developed by a natural person during his or her employment by an entity is subject to a set of different rules. Software copyright initially vests in that employer in the following circumstances:

(a) where the software developed is the foreseen or natural result of carrying out the employee's duty;
(b) where the software results from performing the employee's duty, in accordance with the development objective explicitly assigned in the line of duty; or
(c) where the software is developed through using the funds, exclusive facilities, unpublished exclusive information, or any other material and technical resources of the employer and under its responsibility.

45. In the case where software is developed pursuant to the tasks assigned by a government department, copyright is allocated pursuant to the terms and conditions of the project task document or contract. If not clearly stipulated in that document or contract, the copyright belongs to the organization to which the task was assigned.

§5. Transfer

I. Assignment of Copyright

46. Since the 2001 revision, Chinese Copyright Law allows the outright contractual assignment of copyright. Assignment of the economic rights, in accordance with Article 25 of the Copyright Law, is permissible. Assignment of an economic right of this Law shall require conclusion of a contract in writing, and shall include the following basic clauses:

(a) title of the work;
(b) category and geographic area of the assigned right;
(c) assignment price;
(d) date and manner of payment of the assignment price;
(e) liabilities for breach of the contract; and
(f) any other matters that the contracting parties consider necessary.

II. Licenses

47. Subject to exceptional provisions in the Copyright Law, anyone who exploits the work of another must, in accordance with Article 24 of the Copyright Law, has concluded a licensing contract with, or otherwise obtained permission from, the copyright owner. In any event, remuneration must be provided for exploiting a work.

48. A licensing agreement shall include the following basic clauses:

(a) the category of right licensed for exploitation of the work covered by the license;
(b) the exclusive or non-exclusive nature of the right to exploit the work covered by the license;
(c) the geographic area and term of the license;
(d) the standard of remuneration and the method of payment;
(e) the liability in case of breach of the contract; and
(f) any other matter that the contracting parties consider necessary.

III. Security

49. According to Article 26 in 2010 revision, where a copyright is given as security for an obligation, the parties to the security contract may record it with the National Copyright Administration. The Measure for Recording Copyright-Security Contracts provides that thus recording such a contract preserves the priority, relative to third parties, of the claims which the contract establishes in copyright as security. The first security interest holder to register his security over a copyright takes priority over other security interest holders.

§6. Scope of Exclusive Rights

I. Moral Rights

50. Article 10 of the Copyright Law recognizes each author's rights of making available to the public, of alteration and integrity, and of attribution of authorship. Articles 46 and 47 of the Copyright Law and select criminal provisions further specify acts violating these rights for which civil, criminal, and administrative remedies are available.

51. Right of making available to the public protects the author's interests, such as privacy and creative control, by allowing him or her to decide whether, and how, to make a work available to the public. It grants the author control over any form of making public, for example, through live performance, exhibition, or broadcasting.

52. Right of alteration and integrity covers two rights of 'alteration' and 'integrity'. One is the right to alter, or authorize others to alter, one's work. The other is the right to protect one's work against distortion and mutilation. Article 46(4) of the Law allows for sanctions for 'distorting or mutilating a work created by another'.

53. Right of attribution of authorship is often abbreviated as the 'right of authorship'. It is the right to have authorship correctly and consistently attributed to the actual creator – notably, to have the author's name mentioned on, or in connection with, the work. Further, among the acts for which remedies are provided, Article 47(8) of the Copyright Law specifies 'producing or selling a work where the signature of an author is counterfeited'.

II. Exploitation Rights

54. Article 10 of the Copyright Law enumerates the exploitation rights in the forms of reproduction, distribution, rental, exhibition, public performance, public projection, broadcasting, communication via information network, cinematographic production, adaptation, translation, and compilation.

A. Reproduction Right

55. Reproduction right is the right of producing one or more copies of a work by printing, photocopying, lithographing, making a sound or video recording, duplicating a recording, duplicating a photographic work, or by other means.

B. Performing Right

56. Performing right is the right of publicly performing a work or of communicating the performance of a work by any means to the public. With respect to artistic works, photographic works, or cinematographic works, it is the right of projection that covering making the works reappear to the public by using technical equipment such as a movie or slide projector, disk player, etc.

C. Adaptation Right

57. Adaptation right is the right of creating another original work by changing a pre-existing work.

D. Translation Right

58. Translation right is the right of converting the language of a work into another language. Not only conversion between natural languages but also conversion between computer languages falls into this right.

E. Other Rights

1. *Droit de Suite*

59. Chinese copyright law does not recognize any *droit de suite.*

2. Public Lending Right

60. Chinese copyright law does not recognize public lending right.

3. Other

61. The other rights include:

(a) distribution: the right of providing the original embodiment or copies of a work to the public through selling or issuing gratuitously;
(b) rental: the right of authorizing others, for consideration, temporarily to use a cinematographic work or computer software, except where the computer software is not the essential object of the rental;
(c) exhibition: the right of displaying to the public the original embodiment or a copy of a work of fine art or of photography;
(d) broadcasting: the right of broadcasting a work, or of communicating it to the public by any other means of wireless diffusion, or by wire, or by re-broadcasting the broadcast of the work, or of communicating the broadcast of the work to the public by loudspeaker or any other analogous instrument;
(e) communication via information networks: the right of making a work available to the public by wire or wireless means so that members of the public can access the work from a place and at a time individually chosen by them;
(f) cinematographic production: the right of fixing a work on media by a cinematographic process or a process analogous to cinematography; and
(g) compilation: the right of creating a work by assembling works or parts of works through selection or arrangement.

§7. Limitations or Exemptions to the Scope of Copyright Protection

I. Exempted Use

62. The Copyright Law, Article 22, sets out a list of exemptions. The Internet Regulations, enacted on 18 May 2006 by the State Council, adapt a majority of the exemptions stipulated in Article 22 of the Copyright Law into the network environment:

(a) Private use: Clause 1 of Article 22 allows for the use of a published work for the purpose of the user's own private study, research, or personal entertainment. However, while private end-users may invoke this exception, it remains uncertain whether others, for example, those who merely facilitate private uses, may do so.
(b) Quotation: Clause 2 of Article 22 allows for the use of an 'appropriate' quotation from a published work in one's own work. For a quotation to be 'appropriate', the quotation must be made solely for the purpose of introducing or reviewing the quoted work in question or for clarifying a point. The Internet Regulations permit appropriate quotation from and communication of, via information network, a work that has been made available to the public in one's own work for the purposes of introduction, comment, or illustration.
(c) Education and research: Clause 6 of Article 22 allows for the translation or the limited reproduction of a published work for use by teachers or scientific researchers in classroom teaching or scientific research, provided that the translation or reproduction is not published or distributed. However, such uses may neither interfere with the normal exploitation of the works used nor unreasonably prejudice the legitimate interests of right-holders. Also, this exception has been considered as including, by implication, a teacher's referring to a work and interpreting that work in the classroom. The Internet Regulations permit provision, via information network, in a small quantity of copies, of a work that has been made available to the public for use to a small number of teachers or scientific researchers, in classroom teaching or scientific research.
(d) State uses for official purposes: Clause 7 of Article 22 allows a State organ to use a published work to the extent necessary to fulfil its official duties. The Internet Regulations extend such use to public provision of a work via information network. Such uses may neither interfere with the normal exploitation of the works used nor unreasonably prejudice the legitimate interests of right-holders.
(e) Institutional display or preservation: Clause 8 of Article 22 allows a library, archive, memorial hall, museum, art gallery, or similar institution to reproduce a work in its collection for the purpose of display or preservation. The courts have rejected claims by so-called online libraries, with commercial operations, to benefit from this exception. The Internet Regulations permit provision to the users within the premises by a library, archives, memorial hall, museum, art gallery, or any similar institution of a lawfully published digital work in the institution's collections or a work reproduced in a digital form for the purposes of the display or preservation of the work, provided the work has been damaged or destroyed; is at the risk of being damaged, destroyed, lost, or stolen; is stored in an obsolete format; or is no longer reasonably available in the commercial marketplace.
(f) Translation into minority languages: Clause 11 of Article 22 allows for the translation of a published work from the Han Chinese language into languages of minority nationalities for publication and distribution within the country, if the published work is that of a Chinese citizen, a Chinese legal entity, or other Chinese organization and was originally created in a Chinese language. The

Internet Regulations extend such use to communication via information network.

(g) Braille transliteration: Clause 12 of Article 22 allows for the transliteration of a published work into Braille and for the publication of works so transliterated. The Internet Regulations permit, for the non-commercial purpose, provision via information network, of a literary work that has been made available to the public to the blind people in the way that is perceptible to them.

(h) News reporting: Clause 3 of Article 22 allows for the unavoidable reproduction or use of published works by newspapers, periodicals, radio or television stations, and other mass media if this use is made for the purpose of reporting current events. The Internet Regulations extend such use to communication via information network.

(i) Re-disseminating news articles and speeches: Clause 4 of Article 22 allows newspapers, periodicals, radio or television stations, and other mass media to reproduce or communicate to the public articles already made available to the public by such media on current economic, political, or religious topics, subject to such reservation of rights as the authors may make by express notice on the articles. The Internet Regulations permit provision, via information network, of an article on current issues relating to politics, economics, or religion, provided that it has been available via the information network.

(j) Gratuitous public performance: Clause 9 of Article 22 allows for the gratuitous public performance of a published work, when no fees are charged to the audience and no remuneration is paid to the performers. In the Chinese countryside and cities, ordinary people often gratuitously perform dramatic or musical works in their communities for the purpose of self-entertainment. Those charity performances for which members of the audience pay, but for which the performers receive no payment, do not qualify for this exemption. Nor do performances sponsored by employers for their employees or by local cultural officials for the residents in the regions, where the employer or local cultural official pays the performers, but the performance is free to the audience, qualify.

(k) Artistic works in public places: Clause 10 of Article 22 allows for the copying, drawing, photographing, or video recording of an artistic work located, or on display, in an outdoor public place. The concept of artistic works in an outdoor public place includes artistic works, such as sculptures, paintings, or calligraphy, etc., which are established or displayed in outdoor places for public events. A person should not be liable for reusing a copy, drawing, photograph, or video recording of an artistic work in a reasonable way and within a reasonable scope.

II. Non-voluntary Licensing

63. In addition to exemptions, certain kinds of works may be subject to specified uses without the consent of the authors, but subject to the obligation to pay remuneration:

(a) Reprinting or abstracting works from the press: Article 32(2) of the Copyright Law applies to works published in newspapers or periodicals. Other newspaper or periodical publishers may reprint the work, print an abstract of it, or print it as reference material, but such publishers must pay remuneration to the copyright owners as prescribed in relevant regulations within two months after the work has been used. If the copyright owner wishes to object to the reprinting of his or her work in whole or in part as provided above, he or she is required to provide a notice to that effect at the time when the work is first published in a newspaper or a periodical. If a newspaper or periodical reprints the work without mentioning the author of the work and the newspaper or periodical that initially published the work, it bears liability for resulting damages and should make a public apology.

(b) Mechanical license to record musical works: Under the Copyright Law, where musical works have been legitimately published as sound recordings, such works may be re-recorded and exploited without obtaining consent from the owners of the copyrights but only upon paying them remuneration pursuant to regulation within two months after the works have been used. However, the copyright owners may opt-out of the license by express notice upon publication.

(c) Licenses to broadcast works: In the Copyright Law, there are two non-voluntary licenses that authorize radio and television stations to broadcast published works. Both licenses apply without the possibility for copyright owners to opt-out of them, but subject to the payment of remuneration pursuant to regulation, and both apply to foreign works as well as to Chinese works. The first license allows the broadcasting of all works against remuneration, except recorded works that are subject to the second license and cinematographic works that are specifically excluded from these licenses. The second license allows the broadcasting of works, usually musical works, that have been published and are available as sound recordings; however, it differs from the first license in that it allows for negotiating remuneration with the copyright owners.

(d) License to compile and publish textbooks: The Copyright Law introduces a non-voluntary license allowing for the compilation and publication of textbooks. Within the context of the nine-year compulsory educational plan, parts of published works or short literary texts, musical works, or single works of fine art or photography may be copied, compiled, and published in textbooks without the permission of the copyright owners, who must be remunerated as prescribed by regulations within two months after the works have been used. This license requires that the name of the author and the title of the work subject to the license be mentioned and that the other rights under copyright not be prejudiced. Copyright owners may opt-out of the license by express notice upon publication.

(e) License to distant education: Article 8 of the Internet Copyright Regulations adds a new non-voluntary license allowing parts of published works or short literary texts, musical works, or single works of fine art or photography to be compiled into a courseware, without the permission of the copyright owner, and provided to the registered students via the information network by a distant-educational institution, provided that remuneration is paid to the copyright owner. Copyright owners may opt-out of the license by express notice upon publication.

(f) License to rural use: Article 9 of the Internet Regulations creates another non-voluntary license allowing provision to the public in the rural areas, free of charge, via the information network, of the domestic works on poverty alleviation and for satisfaction of the basic cultural demands (e.g., the works regarding planting and breeding, disease prevention and cure, disaster prevention and relief, etc.), provided that the copyright owners are properly notified and remunerated by the providers. Copyright owners may opt-out of the license by express notice upon publication.

§8. Duration of Protection

64. Article 21 of the Copyright Law only limits the term of the moral right to control the initial making a work available, while Article 20 declares that the other moral rights – that is, the rights of authorship, alteration, and integrity of an author – are unlimited in time.

65. Article 21 of the Copyright Law sets out terms for the economic rights, that is, the rights of exploitation and remuneration, included in copyright. Economic rights generally last for the life of the author plus fifty years. In all cases, the applicable term will end on 31 December of the last year of the term.

66. Special rules apply to the following categories of works:

(a) Photographic and cinematographic works: Article 21 of the Copyright Law sets a term of fifty years, counted from the year of first making public, for the protection of a photographic work or of a cinematographic work, to which is assimilated any work expressed by a process analogous to cinematography. Any such work, however, will no longer be protected fifty years after the year of completion of its creation if it has not been made public within that period of time. The terms of protection for the script, musical work, and other works that are included within a cinematographic work and that can be exploited independently vary according to the copyright owners of these works. If the copyright owner is a natural person, the term of protection is the author's lifetime plus fifty years; if the copyright owner is an entity, the term of protection is fifty years, counted from the year of first making public or, absent making public in that period, from the year of completion.[4]

(b) Works of applied art, computer software: Designs or works of applied art may fall within the category of artistic works, and their term of protection is then as long as that applicable to the other categories of works. The Software Regulations now provide that the term of protection of copyright in software is life plus fifty years or, for software in which an entity initially owns copyright, fifty years counted from the year the software is first made public; however, this term shall

4. Interpretation of several issues relating to the adjudication of, and the application of the Copyright Law to, cases of civil disputes on copyright, adopted at the 1,246th session of the Judicial Committee of the Supreme People's Court on 12 Oct. 2002, effective on 15 Oct. 2002.

lapse fifty years after the year of creation if such software is not made public in that period.

(c) Performances; recordings; broadcasts; editions: Neighbouring rights in a performance, recording, or broadcast last for fifty years from the end of the year in which, respectively, the performance, initial fixation of the recording or broadcast took place. The neighbouring right in a published edition lasts for a ten-year period that begins at the end of the year in which the first publication took place. The performer's neighbouring right to remuneration for a performance used in a recording, or one used in a broadcast programme, lasts as long as the corresponding recording producer's or broadcaster's right.

§9. Neighbouring Rights

67. The Copyright Law and its Implementing Regulations refer to 'rights related to copyright'. These are neighbouring rights enjoyed by performers in their performances, by producers in their audio and video recordings, by radio and television stations in their broadcast programmes, and by publishers in the typographical format of their publications.

I. Performers' Rights

68. The Copyright Law amplifies performers' rights, in relation to their performances, by enumerating the following moral and economic rights that they enjoy:[5]

(a) to claim performance;
(b) to protect the images inherent in their performances from distortion;
(c) to authorize others to make sound recordings or video recordings of their live performances;
(d) to authorize others to reproduce or distribute the sound or video recordings in which their performances are recorded;
(e) to authorize others to make live broadcasts of, or otherwise publicly communicate, their live performances;
(f) to authorize others to communicate their performances to the public via information networks; and
(g) to receive remuneration by exercising any of the economic rights.

II. Producers' Rights

69. The Copyright Law grants producers of sound and video recordings the right to authorize others to reproduce, distribute, rent, and communicate to the public via

5. Copyright Law, Art. 37(1).

information networks their sound or video recordings, and the right to obtain remuneration for such uses.

III. Broadcasters' Rights

70. Aside from copyright in such programmes as constitute works and neighbouring rights in their recordings, broadcasting organizations, that is, radio or television stations, enjoy the following neighbouring rights with respect to the programmes they produce: to fix the broadcasts on audio or video media and to reproduce such fixations, and to re-broadcast their broadcasts.

IV. Publishers' Typographical Design Right

71. Under Article 35 of the Copyright Law, publishers enjoy an exclusive right of exploitation in the typographical design of the books or periodicals they publish. This right arises independently of copyright: for example, the publisher of a new edition of a work, even an old work in the public domain, could assert this right against another party for publishing a copy of its edition.

§10. Infringement and Remedies

I. Principles

72. The General Principles of Civil Law of the People's Republic of China, notably general principles of tort liability, will apply in determining whether a person incurs civil liability for participating in copyright infringement. Specific criminal provisions will determine liability and sanctions in criminal cases. Generally, under Civil Law, copyright infringers are strictly liable for infringing acts.

73. With respect to copyright disputes on the Internet, the Supreme People's Court has articulated guidelines on online liability. In particular, these guidelines provide that Internet intermediaries, such as service and content providers, who participate in copyright infringement via the Internet, or who instigate or assist others in copyright infringement via the Internet, may be held jointly liable for such infringement. Furthermore, liability may be imposed on Internet intermediaries who refuse to take down infringing matter, or who refuse to identify suspected infringers, upon due notice and demand by right-holders.

II. Liabilities of Software End-Users

74. The Software Regulations attenuate such liability for end-users when they reproduce software in either of the following pair of cases:

(a) In one case, the owner of a copy of software has no knowledge, or has no reasonable basis for having knowledge, of the fact that this copy is infringing. In that event, that owner is not liable for damages to the owner of the copyright in the software, but, upon acquiring the requisite level of knowledge, must stop using the software and destroy the infringing copy.
(b) In the other case, the user of the infringing copy would suffer serious damage from stopping use of that copy and from destroying it. In that event, the user of the copy may continue to use the software after paying a reasonable fee to the owner of the copyright in the software.

75. Chinese end-users expressed concern about the extent to which copyright enforcement could lead to searching their computers. The Supreme Court then clarified that the owner of a copy of software will only be liable for copyright infringement in accordance with Article 47(1) of the Copyright Law and Article 24(1) of the Software Regulations when he or she uses the software for a commercial purpose without authorization or otherwise supersedes the scope of his or her license. It is still unclear whether this guideline of the Supreme Court is fully consistent with the Circular on the Prohibition of Use of Illegally Reproduced Computer Software, which provides that entities may not use unauthorized computer software in their computer systems.

III. Civil Remedies

76. Article 46 of the Copyright Law enumerates a large range of acts for which relief may be had in a civil suit brought before a People's Court. Civil remedies are potentially available for the full range of economic and moral rights under copyright and neighbouring rights. In accordance with Article 134 of the General Principles of the Civil Law, a civil court may grant civil remedies for an infringing act, except when the same act has already been sanctioned by the copyright administration.

77. A court may also issue orders to prevent or eliminate the effects of infringement, to compel a public apology, to compel the signing of a pledge of repentance, and to confiscate both the property used in carrying out the illegal infringing activities and the illegal income obtained from these activities. It may also impose fines or detentions as stipulated by law.

78. Article 48 of the Copyright Law sets out the following approaches to assessing monetary awards in cases of infringement of copyright or neighbouring rights:

(a) Actual damages: The amount of damages is normally to be calculated by considering the claimant's actual economic losses. In special cases, the author may be awarded compensation for his moral damages, usually reputational losses.
(b) Illicit gains: Where the losses are hard to calculate and in other special cases, the successful claimant may be compensated based on the infringer's illegal gains.

(c) Statutory damages: In those cases where neither the right-owner's actual losses nor the infringer's illegal gains can be reasonably assessed, the court shall, in light of the circumstances of the infringements, grant the right-owner the damages of up to CNY 500,000.
(d) Costs of stopping infringement: The right-owner's reasonable costs spent for stopping the infringing act shall be included in damages. In accordance with the guidelines of the Supreme Court, the reasonable costs spent by the right-owner include the reasonable fees paid by the right-owner or the agent for investigating the infringements and collecting evidence.
(e) Attorneys' fees: The court may, at the request of the parties or considering the specific circumstances of the case, include in the amount of damages the attorneys' fees that satisfy the provisions issued by the competent authority.

IV. Provisional Measures

79. With respect to civil remedies, provisional injunctive relief may be had from courts both before and after filing suit, while permanent injunctive relief and monetary awards may be had on the close of suit:

(a) Preserving evidence: Where a piece of evidence is likely to be destroyed or lost or difficult to obtain later on, the court may order the evidence to be preserved before any suit is filed.
(b) Temporary restraining orders: Upon hearing satisfactory evidence that infringement is ongoing or imminent and that the applicant's legitimate interests would suffer irremediable damage if the infringement were not immediately stopped, the court may order the cessation of relevant acts and the preservation of relevant property before any suit is filed.

V. Penalties

80. The revised Criminal Code is the main source of criminal remedies and sanctions in China. Its general provisions, for example, Article 225, which defines the crime of 'operating an illegal business', may apply to cases of infringement. Articles 217 and 218 of the revised Criminal Code define the following acts as constituting criminal infringement of copyright or neighbouring rights if they are done with the purpose of obtaining profits and with the knowledge that the acts are criminal:

(a) to reproduce and distribute another person's written work, musical, cinematographic, television or video work, computer software, or other work without the permission of the owner of copyright;
(b) to publish a book to which the exclusive publishing right is enjoyed by another person;
(c) to reproduce and distribute an audio or video recording without the permission of the recording's producer; or

(d) to produce and sell a work of art bearing the forged signature of another person.

81. Infringing reproductions, illegal income and materials, tools and equipment, or other property belonging to the offending entity or individual and used mainly in the crime of copyright infringement may be confiscated.

VI. Administrative Penalties

82. Chinese law empowers administrative organizations to impose sanctions for infringing acts that the Copyright Law enumerates in Article 47. With the 2001 revision, the Copyright Law strengthened such sanctions, which include ordering the cessation of infringing acts, the imposition of fines, and the confiscation of illegal gains, of infringing copies and, in serious circumstances, of materials and devices mainly used to make infringing copies. Where a decision has been made to impose an administrative sanction, any party that objects to it may, within three months of receipt of the written decision, institute proceedings in a People's Court. The copyright administrative authority seeking the sanction may, in the event a party neither institutes proceedings nor implements the decision within the specified time limit, apply to the People's Court for enforcement.

§11. Future Developments

83. Chinese Copyright Law is undergoing the first revision and expected a comprehensive overhaul. The official Draft provided by the National Administration of Copyright is being review at the State Council and will be submitted to the national legislature. The Draft proposes the revisions in the following areas:

- Works of applied art: the Third Draft proposes to add works of applied art as a new category of works, independent of works of fine art. In addition, it proposes to provide uniform legal protection for foreign and domestic works of applied art, and it attempts to address the coordination of multiple intellectual property protections, such as whether a work of applied art in an expired or invalidated patent for a design should be protected in copyright law.
- Moral rights: the Third Draft proposes to merge the right of alteration and integrity – both of the authors' moral rights--because the borderline of the two rights is ambiguous in practice, and alteration is generally accommodated in the right of integrity.
- Economic rights: the Third Draft proposes to restructure the list of exclusive economic rights. It proposes to remove rights of screening, cinematographic production and compilation and to replace the right of broadcasting with an 'extensive' right of communication to cover non-interactive communications by any means, including fixed-time podcasting and streaming on the Internet, while the right of communication via information network remains to cover interactive Internet communications.

- Droit de suite: the Third Draft proposes to add such a remuneration right, under which the author or his/her successor has the right to share the value-added revenue deriving from the resale of the relevant work through public auction, after the first sale of an original work of fine art, a photographic work, or the manuscript of a literary or musical work.
- Joint works: the Third Draft proposes that any individual author of a joint work should have the right to sue for infringement in his/her own name provided that the compensation received therefrom is reasonable and shared among all the authors.
- Works created during employment: the Third Draft proposes to make pervasive changes to the ownership of works created during employment by integrating the current two-type ownership and respecting the parties' autonomy of contracts as to ownership of the relevant works.
- Art in public places: the Third Draft proposes that the property owner of the original of a work of fine art displayed in public places should notify the author in a reasonable time before demolition, destruction or disposal of the original or should otherwise enable the author to protect the copyright through buyback, reproduction or other measures, provided that the original is the sole physical embodiment of the work.
- Term of protection: the Third Draft proposes that the general rules on term of protection be applied to photographic works and works of applied art and proposes that a work be protected for twenty-five years after its completion.
- Three-step test: the Third Draft proposes that an open-ended clause be added to the specific list of limitations or exceptions allowing liability to be excused under 'other circumstances', subject to the TRIPs three-step test.
- Non-voluntary licensing: the Third Draft proposes to reform non-voluntary licensing in the Copyright Law, including narrowing the scope of application and prior registration of non-voluntary licensing. The pending draft for a third revision of the Copyright Law would require that, before any first use under any non-voluntary license, the user would have to register with the pertinent collecting society and pay remuneration within one month after starting its use.
- Orphan works: the Third Draft proposes to issue specific rules to regulate the use of works whose authors either are unidentifiable or cannot be contacted despite the user's diligent search for the authors.
- Neighbouring rights: the Third Draft proposes that performers have right of rental over recordings or copies of recordings of their performances and have remuneration right over their audio-video performances, except as otherwise agreed by both the performers and producers of the audio-video works. It also proposes a new remuneration right for sound-recording producers where a sound recording is disseminated or re-disseminated to the public by wire or wireless means or by way of other technical equipment. In addition, the broadcasting organizations would have more extensive exclusive rights over their broadcasting signals.
- Voluntary registration of copyright transfer: the Third Draft proposes that an exclusive licensee or assignee may register the copyright licensing or assignment agreement with the copyright authority.
- Collective management: the Third Draft proposes to considerably strengthen collective management, although it narrows the scope of application compared with

the previous Draft. It proposes that extended-collective management be applied to the public communication of music or audiovisual works via karaoke systems.
- Safe harbour for network-service providers: the Third Draft proposes that any network-service provider providing 'pure network technical services', such as storage, searches, or links, not be obligated to monitor whether copyright or related rights are being infringed in the process.
- Software end-users: the Software Regulations attenuate strict liability of software end-users when reproducing software without knowledge, or reasonable basis for having knowledge, that this copy is infringing, and provide that they may continue to use the software after paying a reasonable fee to the owner of the copyright in the software, in the case that the user of the infringing copy would suffer serious damage from stopping use of that copy and from destroying it. Upon strong petition of the software industry, the Third Draft proposes to modify the above-mentioned permission for 'continuing use' of the infringing copy. Under the new proposal, the continuing use of the software copy shall be subject to the license of the copyright owner.
- Other proposals: the Third Draft also proposes to reinforce protection for technological-protection measures and rights-management information, to strengthen copyright enforcement measures, such as statutory and punitive damages, and to introduce an administrative mediation system to resolve copyright disputes.

§12. Overlap and Relation to Other Intellectual Property Laws

84. Different Chinese laws govern the following categories of rights: copyrights, design patents, and trademarks. According to the Chinese Patent Law revised for the second time in 2000 and the Chinese Trademark Law revised for the second time in 2001, provisions concerning design patents or trademarks shall not conflict with pre-existing rights, including copyright.

85. After the 2001 revision, the construction or manufacture of industrial products on the basis of drawings or descriptions of engineering or product designs may be considered as 'reproductions'. However, where an engineering or product design that lacks creativity and cannot be characterized as a literary, artistic, or scientific work is drawn or described, no liability will attach to the making of products from such a drawing or description.

86. In China, design patents are also available to protect ornamental and other designs. Such a design patent protects a design against the making of a product based upon it, but it will not automatically arise upon creation. Rather, the Chinese Patent Office must grant the design patent upon the filing of an application and may only do so after determining the novelty of the design. That is, the design to be protected must not resemble, nor be similar to, any design that, before the filing date of the application, has been publicly disclosed in publications, whether in China or abroad; nor may it have been publicly used in China; nor may it conflict with pre-existing rights.

Chapter 2. Patents

§1. Sources: Legislation

87. Patent Law was adopted by the Chinese National People's Congress on 12 March 1984 and came into effect 1 April 1985. It was amended for the first time on 4 September 1992. On 25 August 2000, the second amendment was adopted at the Seventeenth Session of the Standing Committee of the Ninth National People's Congress, and went into effect 1 July 2001. On 27 December 2008, the third amendment was adopted by the Sixth Session of the Standing Committee of the Eleventh National People's Congress, and went into effect 1 October 2009.

88. Implementing Regulations of the Patent were re-promulgated by the State Council on 9 January 2010. They went into effect 1 February 2010 and superseded the Regulations adopted on 15 June 2001. China's Supreme Court issued and then revised the important guidelines concerning application of law in the trials of the disputes on infringements against patent rights. The most recent guidance was issued on 29 January 2015 and effective 1 February 2015.

The State Intellectual Property Office, which is the patent administration under the State Council, published the updated Patent Examination Guidance, effective 1 May 2014.

§2. Patentable Subject Matter

89. In accordance with the Patent Law, patentable 'invention-creations' refer to inventions, utility models, and designs.

90. 'Invention' in the Patent Law means any new technical solution relating to a product, a process, or an improvement thereof. 'Utility model' in the Patent Law means any new technical solution relating to the shape, the structure, or their combination of a product, which is fit for practical use. 'Design' in the Patent Law means any new design of the shape, the pattern, or their combination, or the combination of the colour with shape or pattern, of a product that creates an aesthetic feeling and is fit for industrial application.

91. The stipulations on designs and utility models in the Patent Law are separated from this chapter and explained later in the respective chapters.

§3. Conditions of Patentability

92. Any invention for which patent right may be granted must possess novelty, inventiveness, and practical applicability. 'Novelty' means that the invention is not prior art and that, before the date of filing, no one has filed with the State Intellectual Property Office an application that described the identical invention and was published after the said date of filing. 'Prior art' refers to an identical invention that has been publicly known in the country or abroad through publications, public use, or any other means. 'Inventiveness' means that, as compared with the prior art, the invention has prominent substantive features and represents a notable progress. 'Practical applicability' means that the invention can be made or used and can produce effective results.

93. Applying patent right in any foreign country for an invention completed in China shall be subject to confidentiality examination by the Patent Administration of the State Council. Any violator of the aforementioned requirement may not acquire patent right in China.

§4. Formalities (Procedure for Granting and Obtaining Patent Protection)

I. Applications

94. An applicant for a patent for invention shall file with the State Intellectual Property Office a request, a description and its abstract, and a document of claims. The document of claim shall, on the basis of the description, clearly and briefly define the scope of patent protection.

95. To protect China's rich biological and genetic resources, the Patent Law touches on the issue of genetic resources. According to the Patent Law, no patent shall be granted for any invention or creation that is completed depending on genetic resources, of which the access or use violates provisions of State laws and administrative regulations. Where an invention was completed on the reliance of any genetic resources, the applicant shall state, in the patent application documents, the direct and original sources of the genetic resources. The applicant who cannot identify the original sources must provide the reason.

The impact of this provision on Chinese patent practice depends greatly on how genetic resource will be defined and what will constitute illegal acquisition and use. In the current laws and regulations, the People's Republic of China (PRC) Animal Husbandry Law, Seeds Law, Environmental Protection Law, Law on the Protection for Wild Animals, and the PRC Tentative Regulation on Human Genetic Resources provide regulations/restrictions on acquiring and using animal and human genetic resources (respectively), especially for exporting purposes.

96. Where any foreigner, foreign enterprise, or other foreign organization having no habitual residence or business office in China files an application for a patent in China, the applicant shall be treated under the Patent Law in accordance with the agreement concluded between the country to which the applicant belongs and China, or in accordance with any international treaty to which both countries are parties, or on the basis of the principle of reciprocity. The applicant shall commission a patent agency to legitimately set up the file or handle other patent matters.

97. Where, within twelve months from the date on which any applicant first filed in a foreign country an application for a patent for invention, he, she, or it files in China an application for a patent for the same subject matter, he, she, or it may, in accordance with any agreement concluded between the said foreign country and China, or in accordance with any international treaty to which both countries are party, or on the basis of the principle of mutual recognition of the right of priority, enjoy a right of priority.

98. Where, within twelve months from the date on which any applicant first filed in China an application for a patent for invention, he, she, or it files with the State Intellectual Property Office State Intellectual Property Office an application for a patent for the same subject matter, he, she, or it may enjoy a right of priority.

99. Any Chinese entity or individual may file a patent international application according to the international treaty to which China has acceded. An applicant of a patent international application shall first file an application for patent to the State Intellectual Property Office State Intellectual Property Office.

100. Where two or more applicants file applications for patent for the identical invention-creation, the patent right shall be granted to the applicant whose application was filed first.

II. Examination

101. Where, after receiving an application for a patent for invention, the State Intellectual Property Office, upon preliminary examination, finds the application to be in conformity with the requirements of the Patent Law, it shall publish the application promptly after the expiration of eighteen months from the date of filing. Upon the request of the applicant, the State Intellectual Property Office may publish the application earlier.

102. Upon the request of the applicant for a patent for invention, made at any time within three years from the date of filing, the State Intellectual Property Office will proceed to examine the application as to its substance. The State Intellectual Property Office may, on its own initiative, proceed to examine any application for a patent for invention as to its substance when it deems it necessary.

103. The State Intellectual Property Office may require the patent applicant for an invention that has filed the patent application in a foreign country to submit the material of retrieval used in that foreign country for examining the application or the material of the foreign examination result within the given period; without a justified reason, refusal of submission within the given period would be deemed a withdrawal of the application.

III. Approval

104. With respect to the application for a patent for invention, where it is found after examination as to substance that there is no cause for rejection, the State Intellectual Property Office shall make a decision to grant the patent right for invention, issue the certificate of patent for invention, and register and announce it. The patent right takes effect as of the date of the announcement.

105. Where an applicant for patent is not satisfied with the decision of the Patent Administration rejecting the application, the applicant may, within three months from the date of receipt of the notification, request the Patent Re-examination Board to make a re-examination. The Patent Re-examination Board shall, after re-examination, make a decision and notify the applicant for patent. Where the applicant for patent is not satisfied with the decision of the Patent Re-examination Board, it or he or she may, within three months from the date of receipt of the notification, institute a legal proceeding in the court.

§5. Ownership and Transfer (Assignment: Licenses)

I. Ownership

106. An invention-creation, made by a person in execution of the tasks of the entity to which he or she belongs, or made by him or her mainly by using the material and technical means of the entity, is a service invention-creation. For a service invention-creation, the right to apply for a patent belongs to the entity. After the application is approved, the entity shall be the patentee.

107. With respect to an invention-creation made by a person using the material and technical means of an entity to which he or she belongs, where the entity and the inventor or creator have entered into a contract in which the right to apply for and own a patent is provided for, such a provision shall apply.

108. To prevent the patent ownership disputes later on, it is desirable that employers enter an agreement with employees in advance in respect of the ownership of all work-related inventions.

109. For an invention-creation jointly made by two or more entities or individuals, or made by an entity or individual in execution of a commission given to it or him or her by another entity or individual, the right to apply for a patent belongs, unless otherwise agreed upon, to the entity or individual that made, or to the entities or individuals that jointly made, the invention-creation. After the application is approved, the entity or individual that applied for it shall be the patentee. Unless in the following circumstance, exercise of co-owned patent application right or patent right shall be subject to the agreement of all the co-owners. Where there is no agreement among the co-owners, each co-owner has the right to implement the patent or issue non-exclusive license for any third party to implement the patent; any remunerations deriving thereof shall be allocated among the co-owners.

II. Transfer

110. A patent license agreement shall be in written form, and the licensee shall pay the patentee a fee for the exploitation of the patent. The licensee has no right to authorize any entity or individual, other than that referred to in the contract for exploitation, to exploit the patent.

111. The right to apply for a patent and the patent right may be assigned. The agreement of assignment shall be in written form and registered with the State Intellectual Property Office. The assignment shall take effect as of the date of registration.

112. Any assignment, by a Chinese entity or individual, of the right to apply for a patent, or of the patent right, to a foreigner shall comply with the stipulations of the relevant laws or regulations.

According to the Measures for Recording Patent Right Security Contracts, effective 1 October 2010, where a patent right is given as security for an obligation, the parties to the security contract may record it with the State Intellectual Property Office. The recording such a contract preserves the priority, relative to third parties, of the claims which the contract establishes in patent as security. With the security contract recorded, the patent owner shall not waive the patent right without the consent of the other party; and, any income from the patent licensing or assignment shall be, firstly, used for the payment of the obligation to the other party.

§6. Scope of Exclusive Rights

113. The patentee for an invention, except where otherwise provided for in the Patent Law, enjoys the exclusive right to make, use, offer to sell, sell or import the patented product, or use the patented process, and use, offer to sell, sell, or import the product directly obtained by the patented process for production or business purposes.

§7. Limitations and Exceptions to the Scope of Patent Protection: Compulsory Licenses

I. Non-patentable Items

114. Under the Patent Law, no patent right shall be granted for any of the following:

(a) scientific discoveries;

(b) rules and methods for mental activities;
(c) methods for the diagnosis or for the treatment of diseases;
(d) animal and plant varieties;
(e) substances obtained by means of nuclear transformation; or
(f) inventions violating law or public moral or hampering public interests.

II. Exemption to Patent Infringements

115. According to the Patent Law, none of the following shall be deemed an infringement of the patent right:

(a) where, after the sale of a patented product that was made or imported by the patentee or with the authorization of the patentee, or of a product that was directly obtained by using the patented process, any other person uses, offers to sell, sells, or imports that product;
(b) where, before the date of filing of the application for patent, any person who has already made the identical product, used the identical process, or made necessary preparations for its making or using, continues to make or use it within the original scope only;
(c) where any foreign means of transport that temporarily passes through the territory, territorial waters, or territorial airspace of China uses the patent concerned, in accordance with any agreement concluded between the country to which the foreign means of transport belongs and China, or in accordance with any international treaty to which both countries are party, or on the basis of the principle of reciprocity, for its own needs, in its devices and installations;
(d) where any person uses the patent concerned solely for the purposes of scientific research and experimentation; or
(e) where an entity makes, uses, or imports patented pharmaceuticals or medical devices solely for acquiring information necessary for obtaining regulatory approval, or a third party makes or imports the patented pharmaceuticals or medical devices to that entity.

116. The third amendment of the Patent Law extends the scope of exemptions. Parallel import is explicitly defined as non-infringement, and the Bolar exception is adopted for pharmaceutical related patents.

III. Compulsory Licensing

117. According to the Patent Law and the Measures on Patent Compulsory Licensing (effective 1 May 2012), the State Intellectual Property Office may, in the following circumstances, grant a compulsory license to exploit the pertinent patent.

Where a patent owner failed to sufficiently implement the patent that had been granted three years earlier and for which an application was filed four years earlier, or, where the exercise of patent right was legitimately recognized as a monopoly, for the purpose of eliminating or alleviating the negative impact on competition the

State Intellectual Property Office may upon the request of the entity that is qualified to exploit the invention, grant a compulsory license to exploit the pertinent patent.

Where a national emergency or any extraordinary state of affairs occurs, or where the public interest so requires, the State Intellectual Property Office may grant a compulsory license to exploit the patent for invention under the suggestions of the relevant administrations under the State Council. For the purpose of public health, the State Intellectual Property Office may grant a compulsory license with respect to patents for pharmaceutical products to enable their manufacture and export to other countries or regions, according to the international treaties to which China has acceded.

118. Where the invention for which the patent right has been granted involves important technical advance of considerable economic significance with respect to another invention for which a patent right has been granted earlier and where the exploitation of the later invention depends on the exploitation of the earlier invention, the State Intellectual Property Office may, upon the request of the later patentee, grant a compulsory license to exploit the earlier invention. Where such a compulsory license is granted, the State Intellectual Property Office may, upon the request of the earlier patentee, also grant a compulsory license to exploit the later invention.

119. In ordinary circumstances, compulsory licenses should not be granted unless any entity or individual who applies for compulsory license can prove that a normal license from the patentee has not been obtained within a reasonable period of time on reasonable terms. With respect to patents involving layout-design of integrated circuits, a compulsory license may only be granted for the purpose of public interests or violation of the Monopoly Law.

§8. Duration of Protection: Maintenance and Termination of Patent Protection

120. The duration of patent right for inventions is twenty years, beginning with the date of filing. Patentees shall submit annual maintenance fees to the Patent Administration.

§9. Infringement and Remedies

I. Burden of Proof

121. Where any infringement dispute relates to a patent for invention for a process for the manufacture of a new product, any entity or individual manufacturing the identical product shall furnish proof to show that the process used in the manufacture of its or his or her product is different from the patented process.

II. Doctrine of Equivalence

122. In accordance with the Patent Law, the extent of protection of the patent right for invention shall be determined by the terms of the claims. The description and the appended drawings may be used to interpret the claims.

123. Further, the Supreme Court interprets in the guidelines 2015 that the scope of protection shall be determined by the scope set down by the essential technological feature clearly recorded in the claims, including the scope set down by the technological feature equivalent to the essential technological feature. The equivalent technological feature refers to the technological feature in basically identical means, having basically identical function, resulting in basically identical effect with the technological feature recorded in the claims and capable of being thought of as existing without creative labour by ordinary technicians in that technological field.

124. No infringement shall be found if the alleged infringing product or process belongs to prior art. The Supreme Court interprets in the guidelines that infringing equivalents are limited to equivalents of technical features rather than the whole solution. Where the alleged solution is short of any technical feature recorded in the patent claims, or where any technical feature of the alleged solution is neither identical nor equivalent to any technical feature recorded in the patent claims, the alleged solution shall be deemed non-equivalent to the patent. Any written amendments or statements that restrict the patent scope that the patentee made during the patent prosecution or invalidation proceeding to comply with the granting requirements will have estoppels effects.

III. Innocent Infringements

125. Any person who, for production and business purposes, uses, sells, or offers to sell a patented product or a product that was directly obtained by using a patented process, without knowing that it was made and sold without the authorization of the patentee, shall not be liable to compensate for the damage of the patentee provided that he or she can prove that he or she obtains the product from a legitimate source.

IV. Bad Faith

126. The third amendment of the Patent Law does not address the patentee's liability of bad faith suits. According to the Draft, if the patentee, knowing that the patented invention or design belongs to prior art, still files litigation or administrative action against others, the patentee will be liable to pay damages to the alleged infringer. This revision will reduce the number of bad faith actions that are growing in China.

V. Provisional Measures

127. Confronted with the acting infringement or imminent infringement, any patentee or interested party (such as the licensee of the patent right or the successor of the patentee) may request the court to adopt the measure of pre-proceeding injunction or evidence preservation.

VI. Injunctions

128. Injunctions are the important form of civil remedies against patent infringements. It has been suggested that violation of an injunction be punishable. The suggestion was not adopted by the third amendment.

129. When an application for pre-suit evidence preservation is filed and accepted, the court should make a decision within forty-eight hours and may decide a bond for granting the request. A lawsuit should be initiated within fifteen days from the execution of the evidence preservation, or the evidence will be released.

VII. Damages

130. The amount of compensation for the damage caused by the infringement of the patent right shall be assessed on the basis of the losses suffered by the patentee or the gains that the infringer has gained through the infringement. If it is difficult to determine the losses that the patentee has suffered or the profits that the infringer has gained, the amount may be assessed by reference to one to three multiples of the amount of the exploitation fee of that patent under contractual license. Where no patentee's actual loss, infringer's illegal gains, or licensing fees can be determined, the damages shall be determined, according to the pattern of the acts, infringing nature and circumstances, in the range of CNY 10,000 and CNY 1,000,000.

131. CNY 10,000 and CNY 1,000,000 may be deemed statutory damages granted by the Patent Law.

VIII. Limitation of Civil Litigation

132. Prescription for instituting legal proceedings concerning the infringement of patent right is two years beginning with the date on which the patentee or any interested party obtains or should have obtained knowledge of the infringing act.

133. Where no appropriate fee for exploitation of the invention, subject to an application for patent for invention, is paid during the period from the publication of the application to the grant of patent right, prescription for instituting legal proceedings by the patentee to demand the said fee is two years beginning with the date on which the patentee obtains or should have obtained knowledge of the exploitation of his invention by another person. However, where the patentee has already obtained or should have obtained knowledge before the date of the grant of the patent right, the prescription shall be counted as of the date of the grant.

134. With respect to ongoing patent infringement, the statute of limitations does not apply, and the patentee still has the right to sue after the two-year term expires. Under such circumstances, a court can issue an injunction order, and the damages available for the patentee are limited to damages that occurred in the two years immediately before the filing date of the lawsuit, if infringement is found.

IX. Administrative Punishment

135. According to the Patent Law and the Measures on Patent Administrative Enforcement (effective 1 February 2011), the administrative authority for patent affairs that is handling the patent infringement may order the infringer to stop the infringing act immediately. If the infringer is not satisfied with the order, he or she may, within fifteen days of the date of receipt of the notification of the order, institute a legal proceeding in the court in accordance with the Administrative Procedure Law. If, within the said time limit, such proceedings are not instituted and the order is not complied with, the administrative authority for patent affairs may approach the court for compulsory execution.

136. Where investigating counterfeit patent cases, the Patent Administration may, based on the evidence that has been obtained, examine witnesses and other relevant parties; review and make copies of relevant contracts, receipts, accounting books, and other documents; conduct inspections of premises; seize infringing goods and specialized equipment for infringement; issue orders to stop infringement; and confiscate infringing goods and specialized equipment for infringement in severe cases. However, damages are not available through administrative action. The Patent Administration may order cessation of counterfeit patents, publish the result, confiscate the illegal gains, and impose a fine up to four times the illegal gains. Where there are no illegal gains, the fine shall be up to CNY 200,000.

§10. Overlap and Relation to Other Intellectual Property Laws

137. Computer software is not only a category of copyright work but also subject to patent protection. Invention applications relating to computer programs share common general characteristics with invention applications in other fields. 'Computer programs' mean a coded instruction sequence that can be executed by a device capable of information processing – for example, a computer – so that certain results can be obtained, or a symbolized instruction sequence, or a symbolized statement sequence that can be transformed automatically into a coded instruction sequence. Computer programs per se include source programs and object programs.

138. The invention relating to computer programs refers to solutions for solving the problems of the invention that are wholly or partly based on the process of computer programs and that control or process external or internal objects of a computer by the computer executing the programs according to the previously defined process. The said control or process of external objects includes control of certain external operating process or external operating devices, process or exchange of external data, etc.; the said control or process of internal objects includes improvement of internal performance of computer systems, management of internal resources of computer systems, and improvement of data transmission, etc. Solutions relating to computer programs do not necessarily include changes to computer hardware.

Chapter 3. Utility Models

§1. Sources: Legislation

139. Utility models are one of the patentable categories. Patent Law and the Implementing Regulations are the primary legal sources for their protection.

§2. The Protection of Utility Models

I. Conditions of Protection

140. 'Utility model' in the Patent Law means any new technical solution relating to the shape, the structure, or their combination of a product that is fit for practical use.

141. Any utility model for which patent right may be granted must possess novelty, inventiveness, and practical applicability. Novelty means that the utility model is not prior art and that before the date of filing, no one has filed with the State Intellectual Property Office an application that described the identical utility model and was published after the said date of filing. 'Prior art' refers to an identical utility model has been publicly known in the country or abroad. 'Inventiveness' means that, as compared with the prior art, the utility model has substantive features and represents progress. 'Practical applicability' means that the utility model can be made or used and can produce effective results.

II. Formalities (Procedure for Granting and Obtaining Protection)

142. An applicant for a patent for a utility model shall file a request, a description and its abstract, and a document of claims.

143. With respect to the application for a utility model, where it is found after preliminary examination that there is no cause for rejection, the State Intellectual Property Office shall make a decision to grant the patent right for utility model, issue the relevant patent certificate and register and announce it. The patent right takes effect as of the date of the announcement.

III. Rights and Duration

144. The patentee for a utility model, except where otherwise provided for in the Patent Law, enjoys the exclusive right to make, use, offer to sell, sell or import the patented product, or use the patented process, and to use, offer to sell, sell, or import the product directly obtained by the patented process, for production or business purposes. The duration of patent right for utility models is ten years, beginning on the date of filing.

IV. Limitations, Infringement, and Remedies

145. Patent Law's provisions regarding exemptions to patent infringements, compulsory licenses, liabilities, and remedies are all applicable to the patent for utility models.[6]

146. Where the infringement relates to a patent for utility model, the court or the administrative authority for patent affairs may ask the patentee to furnish a patent assessment report made by the State Intellectual Property Office through searching, analysing, or evaluating the patent.

6. For detailed rules, see Ch. 2, Patents.

Chapter 4. Trademarks

§1. Sources: Legislation

147. Chinese Trademark Law was adopted by the Chinese National People's Congress on 23 August 1982 and came into effect on 1 March 1983. Since its enactment, Chinese Trademark Law has been revised twice: 22 February 1993, and 27 October 2001. The second revision of the Trademark Law was adopted at the Twenty-Fourth Session of the Standing Committee of the Ninth National People's Congress on the same day when the Copyright Law was revised. The second revision, which went into effect on 1 December 2001, updated the level of Chinese trademark legal protection and eliminated the discrepancies between the Trademark Law and the TRIPs Agreement. The Trademark Law was amended for the third time according to the 'Decision on the Revision of the Trademark Law of the People's Republic of China' adopted at the 4th Session of the Standing Committee of the Twelfth National People's' Congress on 30 August 2013. The third revision became effective on 1 May 2014.

148. On 29 April 2014, the State Council promulgated the new Implementing Regulations of the Trademark Law, which went into effect on 1 May 2014, and superseded the prior Implementing Regulations. In addition, the State Administration of Industry and Commerce, the trademark administration under the State Council, published many stipulations on administrative enforcement of trademark right. China's Supreme Court, on 12 October 2002, issued the important guidelines concerning application of law in the trials of trademark disputes.

§2. Protected Subject Matter

I. Signs That May Serve as Trademarks

149. In accordance with the Trademark Law, any word, device, letter, number, three-dimensional symbol, colour combination and sound, or any combination thereof, that identifies and distinguishes the goods of a natural person, legal person, or other organization from those of others is eligible for registration as a trademark.

II. Different Categories of Marks

150. The Trademark Law does not provide any statutory categories of marks. Generally, marks may be divided into characters marks, devices marks, three-dimensional marks, and colour-combinations marks.

151. Collective marks and certificate marks are two special categories of marks. A collective mark refers to the sign registered in the name of an association, institution, or other organization and for the members of the organization to use in commercial activities so as to show the users' membership in the organization. A certificate mark refers to the sign controlled by the organization capable of supervising a kind of good or service but used by entities or individuals outside of the organization on their goods or services so as to certify the source, raw materials, manufacture process, quality, and other characteristics of the goods or services.

§3. CONDITIONS OF PROTECTION

152. Unless the law stipulates otherwise, only registered trademarks are protected by the Trademark Law. A registered trademark shall be so distinctive as to be distinguishable.

I. Banned Signs

153. Under the Trademark Law, the following signs shall neither be used nor registered as trademarks:

(a) those identical with or similar to the State name, national flag, national emblem, national anthem, military flag, army emblem, military anthem or decoration of the People's Republic of China, as well as those identical with the name, symbol or the location of the central organs of the State or the name or device of the symbolizing building in the location;
(b) those identical with or similar to the State name, national flag, national emblem, or military flag of a foreign country, unless otherwise agreed by the foreign country;
(c) those identical with or similar to the flag, emblem, or name of an international intergovernmental organization, unless otherwise agreed by the organization or not likely to mislead to the public;
(d) those identical with or similar to the official signs or hallmarks indicating control and warranty adopted by the competent authorities;
(e) those identical with or similar to the symbols or names of the Red Cross or the Red Crescent;
(f) those having the nature of discrimination against any nationality;
(g) those in the nature of fraud that easily confuses the public with the quality or other characteristics or origins of the goods, or the place of origin of the goods;
(h) those detrimental to socialist morals or customs, or having other unhealthy influences; and
(i) a geographical name as the administrative division at or above the county level and the foreign geographical name well known to the public, unless it has another meaning or is the component of a collective mark or certificate mark.

II. Signs Excluded from Trademark Registrations

154. The signs lack of distinctiveness may be used as trademarks, but cannot be registered with the Trademark Office. The following signs are excluded from trademark registrations:

(a) those merely consisting of the generic names, devices, or types of goods on which the trademark is used;
(b) those merely having direct reference to the quality, main raw materials, function, usage, weight, quantity, or other features of the goods on which the trademark is used;
(c) a three-dimensional sign that merely consists of the shape of a good of its own characteristic, for technological effect or for making the good substantially valuable; and
(d) others that have no distinctiveness.

155. Once the preceding signs acquire distinctiveness through use so as to be distinguishable, they may be registered as trademarks.

§4. Formalities (Procedure for Obtaining Protection and Establishing and Maintaining Trademarks)

I. Applicants for Registration

156. In accordance with the Trademark Law, any natural person, legal person, or other entity, intending to acquire the exclusive right to use a trademark for the goods or to use a service mark for the service, shall file an application for the registration of the mark with the Trademark Office, which is within the State Administration of Industry and Commerce.

157. Two or more natural persons, legal persons, or other entities may jointly file an application for registration of a trademark and jointly enjoy and exercise the exclusive right to use such trademark.

Any application or usage of a trademark shall abide by principles of honesty and credibility.

For goods that must be used in connection with a registered trademark as prescribed by the laws and administrative regulations, a trademark registration must be applied for. Where no trademark registration has been granted, such goods cannot be sold on the market.

The applicant shall indicate on the application the class of goods and describe the goods with which the mark is used, based on the prescribed schedule of classes of goods, and shall file an application. The applicant can apply the same trademark for goods in different classes with an application. The trademark registration applications and other relevant documents can be filed in writing or by other electronic means of data transmission.

An applicant may independently handle trademark registration other trademark matters, and may also authorize a legally established trademark agency to handle trademark matters. Any foreigner of foreign enterprise intending to apply for the registration of a trademark or processing any other trademark matters in China shall commission the trademark agency established according to the law.

A trademark agency shall abide by principles of honesty and credibility, abide by relevant laws and administrative regulations, and handle trademark registration and other trademark matters according to the instructions of its principals; a trademark agency shall also be obliged to keep secret any confidential information and trade or business secrets obtained through the performance of its duties. Where a principal applies for registration of any trademark that may not be registered in accordance with this Law, the trademark agency shall explicitly inform the principal. Where a trademark agency knows or should know that a trademark registration applied for by the principal violates the provisions of on the protection of well-known marks and prior-existing marks with substantive influence, the trademark agency shall not act as an agent for said principal in application for registration of that trademark. Except for applying the use of one's own trademark, a trademark agency shall not register other trademarks in its own name.

II. Right of Priority

158. In accordance with the Trademark Law, any person who has filed an application for registration of a trademark in a foreign country may enjoy, for the purpose of filing the application for registration of the same trademark with respect to the same goods in China, a right of priority within six months of the date of filing of the first application in the foreign country, in accordance with any agreement concluded between China and the foreign country, or the international treaty to which both countries are parties, or the principle of recognition of the right of priority mutually.

159. Where a trademark is used for the first time with respect to goods exhibited at the international exhibition organized or acknowledged by the Chinese government, the applicant for registration of the trademark may enjoy the right of priority within six months of the date of introduction of the goods into the exhibition.

160. Any person desiring to take advantage of the priority shall, when filing the application for registration of the trademark, make a written declaration and submit the documentary evidence.

III. Principle of First Filing

161. Where two or more applicants apply for the registration of identical or similar trademarks for the same or similar goods, the application that was first filed, after examination, shall be preliminarily approved. Where applications are filed on the same day, the preliminary approval shall be given to the trademark that was first used.

162. In accordance with the Trademark Law, any trademark shall not conflict with the other's prior legal right. Thus, an application that was filed first but that conflicts with the other's prior legal right shall not be approved by the Trademark Office.

IV. Examination, Publication, and Opposition

163. An application for trademark registration shall be examined and preliminarily approved by the Trademark Office within nine months from the date of filing the application.

Any holder of prior rights, or interested party who believes that the trademarks violate the provisions of Article 13 paragraph 2, Article 13 paragraph 3, Article 15, Article 16 paragraph 1, Article 30, Article 31, or Article 32, or any person who believes that the trademarks violate the provisions of Article 10, Article 11, or Article 12, may file the opposition within three months from the date of publication of the preliminarily approved trademark in the Trademark Gazette.

Where an opposition is filed against a trademark application published after a preliminary examination, the Trademark Office shall hear the facts and grounds submitted by the opposing party as well as the opposed, shall make a decision on whether or not to approve the application for registration within the twelve months from the date of publication after investigation and verification, and shall notify the opposing party and the opposed of its decision, in writing. If an extension is needed, upon the approval of the State Administration of Industry and Commerce, the time limit can be extended a further three months.

Where no opposition is filed in the designated period, the application shall be approved for registration, a certificate of registration shall issue, and the mark shall be published.

After the expiration of the time limit of opposition, where an applicant fails to apply to the Trademark Office for a review and/or later institute legal proceedings with a People's Court contesting the decision made by the Trademark Review and Adjudication Board, of Trademark Office's decision of rejection of the application or decision of no registration, the Trademark Office's decision shall go into effect.

Where an opposition to a trademark application is rejected, the registration term for a preliminarily approved and published mark shall be counted from the expiry date of opposition period. No retroactive actions may be taken against the others who use an identical or similar mark for the same or similar goods within the expiration date of the opposition period and the date of approval of the application for registration, except that the use with bad faith and causing damage to an applicant.

If an applicant applies to register a trademark used on an identical or similar product that is the same or similar to an unregistered trademark that has been in prior use and the applicant has the prior contractual agreement or business relationship with the prior user, the prior user may file an opposition to the trademark application.

V. Review

164. Where registration is refused and the mark has not been published, the Trademark Office shall notify the applicant of the refusal in writing. Where the applicant is dissatisfied, it may, within fifteen days from receipt of the notification, apply for a review. The Trademark Review and Adjudication Board shall make a final decision within nine months from the acceptance of the application, and notify the applicant in writing. If an extension is needed, upon the approval of the State Administration of Industry and Commerce, the time limit can be extended for a further three months. Where the applicant is dissatisfied with the decision of the Trademark Review and Adjudication Board, it may appeal to the People's Court within thirty days from receipt of the notification.

Where the Trademark Office makes a decision to approve an application for registration, and if the opposing party is dissatisfied with the decision, it may file its dissatisfaction, within fifteen days from the receipt of notification, in writing, to the Trademark Review and Adjudication Board for further review. The Trademark Review and Adjudication Board shall make a review decision within twelve months from the acceptance of the application, and notify the opposed and the opposing party in writing. If an extension is needed, upon the approval of the State Administration of Industry and Commerce, the time limit can be extended for another three months. If the opposing party is dissatisfied with the decision of the Trademark Review and Adjudication Board, it may institute legal proceedings with a People's Court within thirty days from its receipt of notification. The People's Court shall notify the opposing party in the trademark review proceedings, who shall participate in the proceedings as a third party.

In the course of review of the Trademark Review and Adjudication Board, in accordance with the provisions of the preceding paragraph, if determining the relevant prior rights will be based on an outcome determined by a court, or handled by an administrative organization, review for the trademark may be suspended. The proceedings for the review shall resume after the causes of the suspension have been eliminated.

VI. Approval

165. After an application has been published by the Trademark Office, if there is no opposition or if the opposition is finally rejected, the applicant shall acquire the trademark registration.

VII. Trademark Disputes

166. A trademark registration may be cancelled for statutory grounds.

167. According to Article 44 of the Trademark Law, where a trademark registration violates the provisions of Articles 10, 11, and 12 of this Law, or the registration of a trademark was acquired by fraud or any other improper means, the

Trademark Office shall invalidate the registration at issue. Any organization or individual may request that the Trademark Review and Adjudication Board make a ruling to invalidate such a registered trademark.

Where the Trademark Office makes the ruling to invalidate a registered trademark, it shall notify the parties in writing. The parties who refuse to accept the Trademark Office's decision may apply for a review within fifteen days after receiving the decision. The Trademark Review and Adjudication Board shall make its final decision within nine months from its acceptance of the review application, and notify the applicant in writing. If an extension is needed, upon approval of the State Administration of Industry and Commerce, the time limit can be extended for three months. Where the party is dissatisfied with the decision made by the Trademark Review and Adjudication Board, he or she may, within thirty days of receipt of the notification, institute a proceeding in court.

If any organization or individual requests that the Trademark Review and Adjudication Board make a ruling to invalidate such a registered trademark, the Trademark Review and Adjudication Board shall notify the relevant parties after receiving the request, and request them to submit arguments by a specified time. After the Trademark Review and Adjudication Board have made a final ruling either to maintain or to invalidate a registered trademark within nine months from its acceptance of the review application, it shall notify the interested parties accordingly in writing. If an extension is needed, upon the approval of State Administration of Industry and Commerce, the time limit can be extended for three months. Where an interested party is dissatisfied with the ruling of the Trademark Review and Adjudication Board, it may, within thirty days from the receipt of notification, institute legal proceedings in a People's Court. The People's Court shall notify other interested parties in the trademark adjudication proceedings to take part in the legal proceedings as third parties.

Where an opposition is refused and the mark has been approved, the opposing party dissatisfied with the decision may file a request for invalidation of the registered trademark according to the provisions of Article 44 or Article 45 of this Law to the Trademark Review and Adjudication Board.

According to Article 45 of the Trademark Law, where a trademark registration violates the provisions of Articles 10(2) and (3), Article 15, Article 16(1), Article 30, Article 31 or Article 32 of this Law, any holder of prior rights or any interested party may, within five years from the date of registration, request that the Trademark Review and Adjudication Board make a ruling to invalidate the trademark's registration. Where the registration was obtained with bad faith, the owner of a well-known trademark shall not be bound by the five-year limitation.

The Trademark Review and Adjudication Board shall, after receipt of an application for invalidating a trademark, notify the interested parties and request them to submit arguments by a specified time. The Trademark Review and Adjudication Board shall make a final ruling either to maintain or to invalidate a registered trademark within twelve months from the acceptance of the application, and notify the parties in writing. If an extension is needed, upon the approval of the State Administration of Industry and Commerce, the time limit can be extended for six months. Where the interested party is dissatisfied with the ruling of the Trademark Review and Adjudication Board, it may, within thirty days from the receipt of notification, institute legal proceedings in a People's Court. The People's Court shall notify the other interested parties in the trademark adjudication proceedings to take part in the legal proceedings as third parties.

In the course of review for invalidating the announcements of the Trademark Review and Adjudication Board in accordance with provisions of the preceding paragraph, if determining the involving prior rights shall be based on the outcome of judged by the court, or handled by administration organization, review for the trademark can be suspended. The proceedings for review shall resume after the causes of the suspension have been eliminated.

After the expiration of the time limit, where the parties fail to bring suit to a People's Court for a review of invalidating the registered trademark handled by the Trademark Office, or review decisions, decisions on maintaining the registered trademark or decisions regarding invalidating the registered trademark handled by the Trademark Review and Adjudication Board, the decision of the Trademark Office, review decisions or rulings of the Trademark Review and Adjudication Board, shall go into effect.

In the event that a registered trademark is invalidated according to the provisions of Article 44 or Article 45, the invalidation of a registered trademark shall be publicized by the Trademark Office, and the exclusive right to use that trademark shall be deemed as not having existed from the very beginning of proceedings.

A decision or ruling pertaining to the invalidation of a registered trademark shall not be applied retrospectively against prior rulings, nor made and enforced by, the administrative department of industry and commerce concerning trademark infringement cases, or contracts for the transfer of a trademark or for an already enacted licensed use of a trademark. However, if any loss has been caused through the ill will of a trademark registrant to any other party, such loss shall be compensated.

The damages for trademark infringement, transfer fees or royalties for trademark rights, in accordance with the provision of the preceding paragraph, shall be refunded in whole or in part.

A. Absolute Grounds of Cancellation

168. In the following cases, the Trademark Office may cancel the trademark registrations, or the Trademark Review and Adjudication Board may, in accordance with Article 10(2), (3), under the petition of an entity or individual, cancel the trademark registration: the registration violates the stipulation on banned signs, the registration violates the stipulation on signs excluded from registration, or the registration of a trademark was acquired by fraud or any other unfair means.

B. Relative Grounds of Cancellation

169. In the following cases, any trademark owner or interested party may, within five years of the date of registration of the trademark, request the Trademark Review and Adjudication Board to make a decision to cancel such a registered trademark:

(a) the registration conflicts with the legal protection for well-known marks (Article 13, 14 of the Trademark Law);
(b) the registration was applied by the agent or representative in its or his or her own name, without the authorization of the principal or of the person being represented (Article 15 of the Trademark Law);
(c) the registration conflicts with the legal protection for geographical indications (Article 16 of the Trademark Law); or
(d) the registration conflicts with other's prior legal right (Article 31, 32 of the Trademark Law).

170. As for a bad faith registration, no time limit shall be fixed for the owner of a well-known mark to request the cancellation of the mark.

C. *Other Grounds of Cancellation*

171. The registrant of a prior trademark registration who believes the other's trademark registration is identical with or similar to his or her or its trademark registration in the same or similar goods, may, within five years of the date of approval of the other's trademark registration, apply for a review to the Trademark Review and Adjudication Board.

§5. Ownership and Transfer (Assignment: Licenses)

172. A trademark registrant is the owner of trademark right. Where a registered trademark is assigned, both the assignor and the assignee shall jointly file an application to the Trademark Office. The assignee enjoys the exclusive right to use the trademark as of the date the assignment is approved and published by the Trademark Office. To assign a registered trademark, the registrant's all other similar trademarks on the same goods, or the same or similar trademarks on similar goods shall be assigned along with. The Trademark Offices shall not approve any assignment for a trademark, which may cause public confusion or other unhealthy influence, and shall notify the applicant of the reasons for the refusal in writing.

173. A trademark registrant may, by signing a trademark license agreement, authorize other persons to use the registered trademark. Where a party is licensed to use another party's registered trademark, the licensor shall submit the trademark license to the Trademark Office for its records. The Trademark Office shall publish all such records received. A trademark license without recordation with the Trademark Office cannot be used against any third parties.

§6. Scope of Exclusive Rights

174. A trademark registrant is protected by the Law and enjoys the exclusive right to use the trademark with respect to the designated goods or services.

§7. Limitations of the Scope of Trademark Protection

175. Where a registered trademark contains the generic name, device, or type of the goods, or another sign that directly shows the quality, major raw material, function, usage, weight, quantity, or other characteristic of the goods or the geographical name, the trademark registrant shall not prevent others from using the name, word, or device normally.

§8. Use Requirements

176. According to the Trademark Law, the use of trademarks refers to the affixation of trademarks to commodities, commodity packaging or containers, as well as commodity exchange documents or the use of trademarks in advertisements, exhibitions, and for other commercial activities, in order to identify the source of the goods.

Where a trademark registrant alters a registered trademark without approval, the name, address, or other matters concerning the registrant without approval, the Trademark Office shall order it to rectify the situation by a specified time; if they still fail to rectify during the specified time period, the Trademark Office shall cancel the registered trademark.

Where a registered trademark is becoming a generic name in a category of approved goods, or the mark has not been used for a period greater than three years without any justifiable reasons, any organization or individual may request that the Trademark Office make a decision to cancel such registered trademark. The Trademark Office shall make a decision within nine months from its acceptance of an application for the cancellation of a registered trademark due to non-use. If an extension is needed, upon the approval of the State Administration of Industry and Commerce, the time limit can be extended for a further three months.

A party that is dissatisfied with the decision of the Trademark Office to cancel or not cancel a trademark registration may, within fifteen days from receipt of notification, apply to the Trademark Review and Adjudication Board for a review. The Trademark Review and Adjudication Board shall make a final decision within nine months from the acceptance of the application, and notify the applicant in writing. If an extension is needed, upon the approval of the State Administration of Industry and Commerce, the time limit can be extended for a further three months. Where the applicant is dissatisfied with the decision of the Trademark Review and Adjudication Board, it may appeal to the People's Court within thirty days from receipt of the notification.

After the expiration of the time limit, where an applicant fails to apply to the Trademark Office for a review of the office's decision to cancel a trademark's registration, or to institute legal proceedings with a People's Court contesting the review decision of the Trademark Review and Adjudication Board, the decision of cancelling the registration, or review decision, shall go into effect.

A registered trademark that be cancelled shall be publicized by the Trademark Office, and the exclusive right to use the registered trademark shall be terminated from the date of publication.

§9. Duration of Protection, Renewal, and Termination

177. The term of registration of a trademark shall be ten years, beginning with the date of approval of the registration.

Where the registrant intends to continue to use the registered trademark after the expiry of the ten-year period, an application to renew the registration shall be made within twelve months prior to the date of expiration. Where no application for renewal is filed within the six-month period, a grace period of six months is allowed. A trademark registration may be renewed each time for a period of ten years within one day after the expiration of the previous validity time. If no application for renewal is filed at the expiration of the grace period, the registered trademark shall be cancelled. After a trademark registration is renewed, it shall be published.

Where a registered trademark has been cancelled, invalidated or has not been renewed upon expiration, the Trademark Office shall not approve any application for the registration of a trademark that is identical to or similar with the said trademark for a period of one year from the date of cancellation, invalidation, or the date of expiration.

§10. Infringement and Remedies

I. Acts of Infringing Trademark Right

178. Any of the following acts shall be an infringement of the exclusive right to use a registered trademark:

(a) using a trademark that is identical with a registered trademark in connection with the same goods without the authorization of the owner of the registered trademark;
(b) using a trademark that is similar to a registered trademark in connection with the same goods, or that is identical with or similar to a registered trademark in connection with the same or similar goods, without the authorization of the owner of the registered trademark, which may cause public confusion;
(c) to sell the goods that infringes the exclusive right to use the registered trademark;
(d) to counterfeit, or to make, without authorization, representations of a registered trademark of another person, or to sell such representations of a registered trademark as were counterfeited, or made without authorization;
(e) to replace a registered trademark and put into market the goods with respect to which the trademark has been replaced, without the authorization of the trademark registrant;
(f) to intentionally contribute to any others' infringement of the exclusive right to use its registered trademark;
(g) to use any word or device that is identical with or similar to the registered trademark with respect to the same or similar goods, as the designation or decoration

of the goods, without authorization of the trademark registrant, which is so sufficient as to mislead the public;

(h) to provide any person intentionally with facilities such as storage, transportation, post-service, and concealment in his or her infringement against the exclusive right of the trademark registrant;

(i) to deliberately use any word or device that is identical with or similar to the registered trademark or unregistered well-known mark with respect to the same or similar goods as the trade name, without authorization of the trademark registrant, which is likely to cause confusion among the public; and

(j) to register any word or device that is identical with or similar to the registered trademark as the domain name, without authorization of the trademark registrant, and use the domain name for electronic transaction of the related goods, which is likely to cause confusion among the public.

II. Liability of Sale of Infringing Goods

179. Sales of the infringing goods shall be an infringement against the exclusive right of the trademark registrant, regardless of whether the seller has knowledge with respect to the nature of goods. However, where a seller is able to prove that the goods are acquired legitimately and to provide the name of the provider of such goods, it or he or she shall not be liable for damages.

III. Special Protection for Well-Known Marks

180. The State Administration of Industry and Commerce enacted the Stipulations on Recognition and Protection of Well-Known Marks on 3 August 2014. According to the Trademark Law and the Stipulations, should any rights of a trademark well known to the relevant public be infringed, the trademark holder can follow the relevant provisions in the Trademark Law to request the protection of the well-known trademark. However, a producer or operator shall not use the words 'Well-Known Trademark' on its goods, packaging, or container, or in its advertising, exhibitions or other commercial activities.

181. Where a trademark constitutes a reproduction, an imitation, or a translation, liable to create confusion, of another's well-known mark unregistered in China and used for identical or similar goods, it shall not be registered, and the use of such mark shall be liable for trademark infringement.

182. Where a trademark constitutes a reproduction, an imitation, or a translation of another's well-known mark having been registered in China and used for goods or services that are not similar to those with respect to which the trademark is used, it shall not be registered, and the use of such mark shall be liable for trademark infringement – provided that use of that trademark would mislead the public and provided that the interests of the owner of the registered well-known mark are likely to be damaged by such use.

183. A well-known trademark, based on the parties' request, can be recognized by the courts in the relevant case should such a recognition is needed for the investigation of the fact of the case. The following elements shall be taken into account for recognition of a well-known mark:

(a) knowledge of the trademark in the relevant sector of the public;
(b) duration of use of the trademark;
(c) duration, degree, and geographical scope of any promotion for the trademark;
(d) record showing that the trademark has been protected as a well-known mark; and
(e) other elements proving the reputation of the trademark.

In examining a trademark registration and in the course of investigating cases involving illegal use of trademarks handled down by the authorities for industry and commerce may, upon a claim filed by the parties involved in accordance with the Trademark law, the Trademark Office may make a determination as to whether a trademark is a well-known trademark.

In the process of handling a trademark dispute, the parties may, in accordance with the Trademark Law make such claims in regard to whether a trademark is well known; The Trademark Review and Adjudication Board may, in accordance with the needs of a specific case, make a determination as to whether a trademark is well known.

IV. Legitimate Use

184. An exclusive rights holder of a registered trademark shall have no right to prohibit other people from making justifiable use of the common name, logo or model contained in the relevant registered trademark or the quality, principal raw materials, functions, uses, weight, quantity, geographic name or other features that are explicitly expressed in the registered trademark.

Where three-dimensional registered trademarks are by the product's own nature essentially the shape of the product, and provide the goods bearing the mark with a specific value, a trademark holder shall have no right to prohibit other parties from reasonably using a similar shape to realize a similar special or technical effect.

Where an identical or similar trademark has been used in connection with the same goods or similar goods by others before the registrant's application, the exclusive right holder of said registered trademark shall have no right to prohibit other people from using the aforesaid trademark from continuous use of such trademark within the original scope, but may request its users to add proper marks for distinction.

V. Civil Remedies

185. In accordance with the Trademark Law, the court may take the measures of pre-proceeding property preservations, pre-proceeding injunctions, and pre-proceeding evidence preservation.

186. The forms of civil liability for trademark infringement include cessation of infringement, removal of obstacle, elimination of danger, compensation for loss, elimination of ill effect, etc. The amount of damages for infringing the exclusive right to use a trademark shall be actual losses that the right owner has suffered as a result of the infringement during the period of the infringement; where the losses suffered by the right owner cannot be determined, the amount of damages for trademark infringement shall be the profits that the infringer has earned as a result of the infringement during the period of the infringement; where the losses suffered by the right owner, or the profits earned by the infringer, cannot be determined, the amount of damages shall be determined based on a reasonable amount that would be paid for a licensing royalty for the trademark right. If there is malicious infringement and an existence of serious circumstances, the amount may be more than one up to three times the aforesaid determined amount. The amount of damages will also include reasonable expenses the right owner has suffered to prevent the infringement.

For the purpose of determining the amount of damages, where the account books and information related to the infringement are held by the infringer, and where the rights owner has presented as much proof of its claims as is practically possible, a People's Court may order the infringer to submit such account books and information. If the infringer refuses to submit such account books and information, or submit a false version thereof, a People's Court may determine the amount of damages with reference to the right owner's claims and proof.

Where the actual losses suffered by the right owner, the profits earned by the infringer, or the licensing royalties of trademark infringement cannot be determined, a People's Court shall award damages up to RMB 3,000,000, depending on the facts of the case.

VI. Administrative Enforcement

187. Where the Administration of Industry and Commerce, under the request of a trademark registrant or interested party to handle a trademark infringement dispute, considers that the trademark infringement is established, it may order the infringer to stop the infringing act immediately, may seize or destroy the infringing goods and the tools or equipment specifically used to produce the infringing goods or counterfeit representations of the registered trademark, and may impose a fine.

If the amount of illegal earnings is greater than RMB 50,000, a fine up to five times the amount of the illicit earnings may be imposed; if there is no illicit business revenue, or the total amount of illicit business revenue is less than RMB 50,000, a fine up to RMB 250,000 may be imposed; if trademark infringement occurs more than two times within a period of five years or other serious circumstances, a severe punishment shall be given. Where a seller with no knowledge of its infringing goods can prove the legality of acquiring such goods and point out the provider, the administration of industry and commerce shall order the seller to cease selling its goods and the latter may be ordered to stop selling the infringing goods.

If any party is not satisfied with the decision, it or he or she may, within fifteen days of the receipt of the notification of the decision, institute a legal proceeding in the court in accordance with the Administrative Procedure Law. If, within the said time limit, the infringer neither institutes such a proceeding nor complies with the order, the Administration of Industry and Commerce may approach the court for compulsory execution.

Upon dispute of the amount of damages arising from infringing the exclusive right of the trademark, the parties involved may request the administration of industry and commerce to mediate in settling the amount of damages, or may appeal to a People's Court in accordance with the Civil Procedure Law of the People's Republic of China.

Upon the process of investigating activities suspected of having infringed upon another party's exclusive right to use a registered trademark, where any dispute arises with respect to the ownership of the trademark, or the right owner files lawsuits of trademark infringement to a People's Court, the administration of industry and commerce may suspend the aforesaid process. The proceedings for review shall resume or stop after the causes of the suspension have been eliminated.

188. In accordance with the Trademark Law, the State Administration of Industry and Commerce at or above the county level may, on the basis of the evidence of suspected violation of the Law or the report, exercise the following powers to investigate the suspected acts of infringements against a registered trademark:

(a) to inquire of the relevant parties, and investigate the facts relevant to the infringement against the registered trademark;
(b) to examine or reproduce the parties' contracts, invoices, account books, and any other materials relevant to the infringing acts;
(c) to search the place in which the party is suspected to commit infringement against the registered trademark; and
(d) to check up the articles related to the infringing act and to order to seal or hold the articles that have been proved by evidence to be infringing to the registered trademark.

VII. Penal Punishments

189. In accordance with the Trademark Law and the Criminal Law, the following cases are so serious as to constitute a crime; the infringer shall be prosecuted for its or his or her criminal liabilities in addition to providing compensation for the damages suffered by the infringed:

(a) where any party uses a trademark that is identical with or similar to a registered trademark with respect to the same or similar goods without the authorization of the proprietor of the registered trademark;
(b) where any party counterfeits, or makes without authorization, representations of a registered trademark of another person, or sells such representations of a registered trademark as were counterfeited or made without authorization; and
(c) where any party knowingly sells the infringing goods.

§11. Overlap and Relation to Other Intellectual Property Laws

190. According to the Trademark Law, provisions concerning trademarks shall not conflict with pre-existing rights, including copyright. If the trademark right conflicts with the copyright in a pre-existing work, the copyright shall prevail. Consider the case in which, after the 2001 revision of the Trademark Law, a painting is pirated and registered as a trademark. The trademark registration may then be cancelled at the request of the copyright owner of the painting.

Chapter 5. Trade Names

§1. Sources: Legislation

191. The Law Against Unfair Competition was adopted at the Third Session of the Standing Committee of the Eighth National People's Congress on 2 September 1993, effective since 1 December 1993. The State Administration for Industry and Commerce (SAIC) has formulated the draft of the revised Law against Unfair Competition because the current law has become incompatible with the economic development, and it is necessary to make amendments. It is suggested by National People's Congress Financial and Economic Committee that SAIC should accelerate the amendment process and submit the draft to the Standing Committee of National People's Congress for discussion as early as possible.

192. On 17 January 2007, the Supreme People's Court promulgated the Judicial Interpretation on Several Issues Relating to Law Application to the Civil Trial of Unfair Competition Cases, which is the first judicial interpretation on the trial of unfair competition cases since the promulgation of Law Against Unfair Competition in 1996.

193. In accordance with the Law Against Unfair Competition, any act of a business operator who, in transactions in the market, violates the principle of voluntariness, equality, fairness, honesty, and credibility, and that fails to observe generally recognized business ethics, constitutes unfair competition. In accordance with the Law Against Unfair Competition, infringements against trade names are one of the categories of unfair competition regulated by this Law.

§2. The Protection of Trade Names

194. Under the Law Against Unfair Competition, the act of using, without authorization, the business name or personal name of another person on his or her own goods, leading people to mistake them for the goods of the other person, constitutes unfair competition.

195. Where an operator carries out any act of unfair competition and causes damage to the injured operator, he or she shall bear responsibility for compensating the damages. Where the losses suffered by the injured operator are difficult to calculate, the amount of damages shall be the profits gained by the infringer during the period of infringement through the infringing act. The infringer shall also bear all reasonable costs paid by the injured operator in investigating the acts of unfair competition committed by the operator suspected of infringing his or her lawful rights and interests.

196. Where the lawful rights and interests of the injured operator are damaged by the acts of unfair competition, he or she may institute proceedings before a People's Court.

Chapter 6. Industrial Designs

§1. Sources: Legislation

197. Industrial designs are one of the patentable subject matters. The Patent Law and the Implementing Regulations are the primary legal sources for their protection.

§2. Protected Subject Matter

198. 'Design' in the Patent Law means any new design of the shape, the pattern, or their combination, or the combination of the colour with shape or pattern, of a product that creates an aesthetic feeling and is fit for industrial application.

§3. Conditions of Protection

199. Any design may be granted for patent right provided that it does not belong to any prior design and there is no application identical with and similar to any design that, before the date of filing, has been filed with the Patent Administration of the State Council and recorded in the patent application documents published after the date of filing. 'Prior designs' refer to the designs that have been known to the public before the date of filing. A patentable design must show significant difference from any prior design or element combination of any prior design and must not be in conflict with any prior right of any other person.

200. The additional requirement on difference from element combination of prior designs is somewhat like the inventiveness requirement for inventions and utility models. Furthermore, no patent shall be granted for planar printings whose design pattern, colour, or their combination plays only an identification function. Obviously, the threshold for design patents becomes higher, and so-called junk design patents will be excluded.

§4. Formalities (Procedure for Granting and Obtaining Protection)

201. An applicant for a patent for design shall file with the State Intellectual Property Office a request, drawings or photographs of the design, and a brief description of the design.

202. The third amendment of the Patent Law provides new provisions for designs. First, the optional brief description of the design under the current rules becomes compulsory for design applications, and the document may be used to interpret the drawings or photos when constructing the scope of protection of the design patents. Second, a design application for multiple similar designs of a product becomes possible.

203. Within six months from the date on which any applicant first filed in a foreign country an application for a patent for design, or from the date he, she, or it files in China an application for a patent for the same subject matter, he, she, or it may – in accordance with any agreement concluded between the said foreign country and China, or in accordance with any international treaty to which both countries are party, or on the basis of the principle of mutual recognition of the right of priority – enjoy a right of priority.

204. With respect to the application for a design, where it is found after preliminary examination that there is no cause for rejection, the State Intellectual Property Office shall make a decision to grant the patent right for design, issue the relevant patent certificate, and register and announce it. The patent right takes effect as of the date of the announcement.

§5. Ownership and Transfer (Assignment: Licenses)

205. The Patent Law's provisions regarding ownership and transfer are applicable to the patents for designs.[7]

§6. Scope of Exclusive Rights

206. The patentee for a design enjoys the exclusive right to make, sell, offer to sell, or import the product incorporating its or his or her patented design for production or business purposes.

§7. Limitations of the Scope of Protection

207. The Patent Law provisions regarding exemptions to patent infringement are applicable to the patents for designs.[8] Compulsory licenses, however, shall not be applied to the patents for designs.

§8. Duration of Protection

208. The duration of patent right for designs is ten years as of the date of filing.

§9. Infringement and Remedies

209. The Patent Law provisions regarding infringement and remedies are applicable to the patents for designs.[9]

7. For detailed rules, see Ch. 2, Patents.
8. For detailed rules, see Ch. 2, Patents.
9. For detailed rules, see Ch. 2, Patents.

§10. Overlap and Relation to Other Intellectual Property Laws

210. Designs are patentable as well as copyrightable. Different from the automatic protection of copyright, designs are not protected under the Patent Law unless approved by the Patent Administration. In addition, duration of patent protection for design is much shorter than that of copyright protection.

Chapter 7. Plant Variety Protection

§1. Sources: Legislation

211. The Regulations on Protection of New Varieties of Plants was enacted by the State Council on 20 March 1997 and went into effect on 1 October 1997. The Regulations were revised by the State Council on 31 January 2013 and the revision became effective 1 March 2013.

212. Implementing Rules for the Regulations on the Protection of New Varieties of Plants (Agriculture Part) were promulgated by the Ministry of Agriculture on 27 April 1999. The Implementing Rules for the Regulations on the Protection of New Varieties of Plants (Forest Part) were promulgated by the Ministry of Forestry on 16 June 1999.

213. On 12 January 2007, the Supreme People's Court promulgated the 'Several Provisions of the Supreme People's Court on Issues Relating to Application of Law to Trial of Dispute Case over New Plant Variety' (Several Provisions), effective 1 February 2007.

§2. Protected Subject Matter

214. The protected plant variety refers to a cultivated plant variety, or a developed one based on a discovered wild plant, that is new, distinct, uniform, and stable and whose denomination is adequately designated.

§3. Conditions of Protection

215. Any plant variety for which variety rights are granted shall have the characteristic of novelty. 'Novelty' means that the propagating material of the new plant variety for which application of variety rights has been made has not been sold prior to the filing date of the application, or has not been for sale, with the consent of the breeder, for more than one year within the territory of China; the propagating material of vines, forest trees, fruit trees, and ornamental plants must not have been for sale for more than six years, or the propagating material of other plant varieties for more than four years, in a foreign territory.

216. Any plant variety for which variety rights are granted shall have the characteristic of distinctness. 'Distinctness' means that the plant variety for which application of variety rights has been made must noticeably distinguish it from any other plant variety known prior to the filing of the application.

217. Any plant variety for which variety rights are granted shall have the characteristic of uniformity. 'Uniformity' means that the plant for which application of variety rights has been made is uniform, subject to the variation that may be expected, in its relevant features or characteristics after propagation.

218. Any plant variety for which variety rights are granted shall have the characteristic of stability. 'Stability' means that the plant variety for which application of variety rights has been made keeps its relevant features or characteristics unchanged after repeated propagation or at the end of a particular cycle of propagation.

219. Any plant variety for which variety rights are granted shall have an adequate denomination, which shall be distinguishable from that for any other known plant variety of the same or similar botanical genus or species. The denomination, after its registration, shall be the generic designation of the new plant variety in question. The following shall be avoided in the selection of a denomination for a new variety:

(a) those consisting of only numbers;
(b) those violating social morals; and
(c) those liable to mislead as to the features or characteristics of the new plant variety, or the identity of the breeder.

§4. Formalities (Procedure for Granting and Obtaining Protection)

I. Applications

220. Where Chinese entities and persons apply for variety rights, they may file an application with the examining and approving authorities directly or through a representative agency commissioned for the purpose. Where the new plant variety for which Chinese entities and persons apply for variety rights involves national security or major interests and therefore needs to be kept confidential, it shall be dealt with in accordance with the relevant national regulations.

221. If a foreigner, a foreign enterprise, or any other foreign institution files an application for variety rights in China, the application shall be handled under these Regulations in accordance with any agreement concluded between the country to which the applicant belongs and China, or any international convention to which both countries are party, or on the basis of the principle of reciprocity.

222. For the purposes of applying for variety rights, an application and specification conforming to the prescribed forms, as well as a photograph of the variety, shall be submitted to the examining and approving authorities, which are the Agriculture or Forestry Administration of the State Council.

223. One new plant variety shall be granted only one set of variety rights. If two or more applicants apply separately for variety rights with respect to the same new plant variety, the variety rights shall be granted to the person who applies first; in the case of a simultaneous application, the variety rights shall be granted to the person who has first accomplished the breeding of the new plant variety concerned.

II. Examination

224. The examining and approving authorities shall complete the preliminary examination within six months after the variety rights application is formally received. Where the variety rights application is found acceptable on preliminary examination, the examining and approving authorities shall have it published within three months.

225. The examining and approving authorities shall then carry out a substantive examination of the distinctness, uniformity, and stability of the variety for which application of variety rights has been made.

226. The examining and approving authorities shall conduct the substantive examination on the basis of application documents and other relevant written information. Where they deem it necessary, the examining and approving authorities may entrust a designated testing institution with undertaking tests or with inspecting the results of growing tests or other trials that have already been carried out.

227. For the purposes of examination, the applicant shall, at the request of the examining and approving authorities, furnish necessary information and the propagating material of the new plant variety in question.

III. Approval

228. Where the variety rights application is found to be in conformity with the provisions of these Regulations on substantive examination, the examining and approving authorities shall make a decision to grant the variety rights, issue the new variety rights title, and have it registered and published.

IV. Re-examination

229. The examining and approving authorities shall set up a Re-examination Board for New Varieties of Plants.

230. Where any applicant is not satisfied with the decision of the examining and approving authorities refusing a variety rights application, that applicant may, within three months of the date of receiving the notification, request that the Re-examination Board for New Varieties of Plants to carry out a re-examination. The Re-examination Board for New Varieties of Plants shall, within six months of the date of receiving the request for re-examination, make a decision and notify the applicant accordingly.

231. Where any applicant is not satisfied with the re-examination decision of the Re-examination Board for New Varieties of Plants, that applicant may, within fifteen days of the date of receiving the notification, file a suit with the People's Court.

§5. Ownership and Transfer (Assignment: Licenses)

232. The entity that, or the person who, has accomplished the breeding has an exclusive right to their protected variety.

233. In the case of job-related breeding accomplished by any person in undertaking tasks for the entity to which he or she belongs, or primarily by using the facilities of that entity, the right to file an application for variety rights with respect to the new plant variety shall belong to the entity in question; for breeding that is not job-related, the right to file such an application shall belong to the person accomplishing the breeding. Upon approval of the application, the variety rights shall belong to the applicant.

234. For commissioned breeding or jointly conducted breeding, the ownership of the variety rights shall be agreed upon by the parties in a contract; failing such an event, the variety rights shall belong to the entity or person commissioned to conduct or jointly conduct the breeding.

235. The right to file an application for variety rights with respect to a new plant variety and the variety rights may be assigned in accordance with the law.

236. If a Chinese entity or person wishes to assign to a foreigner the right to file an application or the variety rights with respect to a new plant variety bred in China, such assignment shall be approved by the examining and approving authorities.

237. In the case of an assignment within China of the right to file an application or of the variety rights by a State-owned entity, it shall be submitted in accordance with the relevant national regulations for approval by the competent administrative departments concerned.

238. The parties involved in the assignment of the right to file an application or of the variety rights shall submit a written contract, and shall register the assignment before the examining and approving authorities, which in turn shall publish the assignment.

§6. Scope of Exclusive Rights

239. Except otherwise provided in these Regulations, no other entity or person shall, without the consent of the holder of the variety rights, produce or sell for commercial purposes the propagating material of the said protected variety, or use for commercial purposes the propagating material of the protected variety in a repeated manner in the production of the propagating material of another variety.

240. Regardless of whether or not the term of the protection of the protected variety has expired, the denomination of the protected variety as used in its registration must be used for sales thereof.

§7. Limitations of the Scope of Protection: Compulsory Licenses

I. Exemptions

241. Without prejudice to other rights of the variety rights-holder under these Regulations, the exploitation of the protected variety shall not require authorization from, or payment of royalties to, the variety rights-holder for the following purposes:

(a) exploitation of the protected variety for breeding and other scientific research activities; and
(b) the use for propagating purposes by farmers, on their own holdings, of the propagating material of the protected variety harvested on their own holdings.

II. Compulsory Licensing

242. The examining and approving authorities may, in the national or the public interest, decide to grant a compulsory license to exploit new plant varieties, which should be subsequently registered and published.

243. The entity that, or the person who, is granted a compulsory license for exploitation shall pay the variety rights-holder a reasonable exploitation fee, the amount of which shall be fixed by consultation between the two parties. Where the parties fail to reach an agreement, the examining and approving authorities shall adjudicate.

244. Where the variety rights-holder is not satisfied with the decision to grant a compulsory license or is not satisfied with the adjudication regarding the fee payable for exploitation, he, she, or it may, within three months of the date of receiving the notification, file a suit with the People's Court.

III. Termination of Rights

245. Variety rights shall be terminated prior to the expiration of the term thereof in any of the following cases:

(a) where the variety rights-holder makes a written statement renouncing his or her variety right;
(b) where the variety rights-holder has not paid the annual fees as prescribed;
(c) where the variety rights-holder has not furnished, in the manner required by the examining and approving authorities, such propagating material of the protected variety necessary for control; and
(d) where, on control, the protected variety no longer conforms to the features and characteristics that existed when the variety rights were granted.

246. The termination of the variety rights shall be registered and published by the examining and approving authorities.

§8. Duration of Protection

247. The term of protection of variety rights, beginning with the date of grant thereof, shall be twenty years for vines, forest trees, fruit trees, and ornamental plants and fifteen years for other plants.

248. The variety rights-holder shall pay annual fees from the year in which the variety rights are granted, and shall furnish propagating material of the protected variety for the purposes of control as required by the examining and approving authorities.

§9. Infringement and Remedies

I. Liabilities and Civil Remedies

249. The Supreme People's Court's Several Provisions define two types of infringement acts related to new plant variety and provide the standards for judgment of the infringing acts. Where the feature and nature of the alleged article identical or not identical with the feature and nature of the claimed variety is caused by non-genetic mutation, the courts shall identify the alleged article as propagation material of the granted variety manufactured or sold for commercial purpose. Where alleged infringers repeatedly use the propagation material of the granted variety as a parent to propagate with another parent, the courts shall deem the act as repeatedly using propagation material of the granted variety for the production of another variety.

250. After the variety rights have been granted, for the period beginning with the date on which an acceptable application is published on preliminary examination and ending with the date of a grant of variety rights, the variety rights-holder is entitled to claim compensation from an entity that, and an person who, has produced or sold the propagating material of the protected variety in question for commercial purposes without his or her consent.

251. The Several Provisions also provide regulations on institutions and methods of appraisal where expertise appraisal is necessary in the trial of dispute case over new plant variety.

252. According to the Several Provisions, where the rights-holder files a request for stopping the infringing act in advance or preserving evidence when instituting a proceeding, the court may make a decision on the request in advance after examination.

253. With regard to the liabilities, the court shall issue orders of stopping the damages and paying for the losses. Upon the request of the right-holder, the court may determine the amount of the damages according to the profit obtained by the infringer or the losses suffered by the right-holder. The court may also determine the amount on the basis of royalties as requested by the right-holder. Where the amount is difficult to determine, a statutory amount of less than CNY 500,000 can be ordered.

254. Regarding the disposal of infringing plants, the Several Provisions propose that, where the infringing plants are still in growth or the destroying of infringing plants may result in adverse effects, the court may not order the infringer to destroy the infringing plants. Where farmers accept another's offer to breed the infringing plants and do not knowingly commit the act of infringement, the farmers should not bear liability for compensation.

II. Administrative Penalties

255. Where the propagating material of the protected variety is produced or sold for commercial purposes without the consent of the variety rights-holder, the variety rights-holder or the party having an interest therein may request the administrative departments of agriculture and forestry of the People's Governments at provincial level or above to handle it in accordance with their respective competence, if the right-holder does not want to directly file a suit with the People's Court.

256. Where any new plant variety is counterfeited, the administrative departments of agriculture and forestry of the People's Governments at county level or above shall order the party concerned to stop the counterfeiting act, confiscate the unlawful earnings and the propagating material of the plant variety, and punish him or her with a fine of at least one but not exceeding five times more than the unlawful earnings; where the circumstances of the case are so serious as to constitute a crime, the party concerned shall be subjected to a criminal liability investigation in accordance with the law.

257. Where the protected variety is sold without using the denomination as used in its registration, the administrative departments of agriculture and forestry of the People's Governments at county level or above shall, in accordance with their respective competence, order a correction within a specified time limit, and may impose a fine not exceeding CNY 1,000.

258. The administrative departments of agriculture and forestry of the People's Governments at provincial level or above may, according to their respective competence and based on the principle of free will of the parties, mediate the compensation of damages caused by the infringement. Where accord has been reached through mediation, it should be executed by the parties concerned; where no accord has been reached through mediation, the variety rights-holder or the party having an interest therein may file a suit with the People's Court according to civil action procedures.

259. In handling cases of infringement or counterfeit of variety rights in accordance with their respective competence, the administrative departments of agriculture and forestry of the People's Governments at provincial level or above may, for the purposes of safeguarding the public interest of the society, order the infringer to stop the infringing act, confiscate the unlawful earnings, and punish him or her with a fine not exceeding CNY 250,000 provided that the value of the goods is less than CNY 50,000, or impose a fine one to five times of the goods value provided that the value is more than CNY 50,000.

§10. Overlap and Relation to Other Intellectual Property Laws

260. Legal protection for plant varieties is similar to but independent of the patent system. Under the Patent Law, no patent right shall be granted for plant varieties. Therefore, patent system and the sui generis system for plant varieties are not overlapping.

Chapter 8. Chip Protection

§1. Sources: Legislation

261. The Regulations on Protection of Layout Designs of Integrated Circuits and its Implementing Regulations were enacted on 19 April 2001 and went into effect 1 October 2001.

§2. Protected Subject Matter

262. In accordance with the Regulations, a layout-design of an integrated circuit may be registered with the State Intellectual Property Office (SIPO). An 'integrated circuit' means a semiconductor integrated circuit, that is, a product, in its intermediate or final form, that uses semiconductor material as its chip, in and/or on which two or more elements, at least one of which is an active element, and some or all of the interconnections are integrally formed and that is intended to perform a certain electronic function. 'Layout-design' of an integrated circuit means the three-dimensional disposition of the two or more elements, at least one of which is an active element, and some or all of the interconnections of an integrated circuit, or such a three-dimensional disposition prepared for the manufacture of an integrated circuit.

§3. Conditions of Protection

263. A protected layout-design shall be original – that is, the intellectual creation of the creator – and shall not be the routine design generally acknowledged by layout-design creators and integrated circuits manufacturers.

264. Layout-designs created by Chinese citizens, legal persons, and other entities and the layout-designs created by foreigners but first put into commercial exploitations within the territory of China are protectable under the Regulations. Other layout-designs created by foreigners may also enjoy legal protection in accordance with the bilateral agreements on protection of layout-designs between China and the foreign countries or the international treaty on layout-designs to which China and the foreign countries are parties.

§4. Formalities (Procedure for Granting and Obtaining Protection)

265. Where an application for registration of layout-design is filed, the following shall be submitted to the Intellectual Property Administration Department of the State Council:

(a) an application form for registration of layout-design;
(b) a copy or drawing of the layout-design;

(c) where the layout-design has been put into commercial exploitation, a sample of that integrated circuit incorporating the layout-design; and
(d) other materials required by the Intellectual Property Administration Department of the State Council.

266. Where a layout-design for which registration is applied relates to the security or other vital interests of the State and is required to be kept secret, the application shall be handled in accordance with the relevant provisions of the State.

267. Any layout-design, if no application for its registration has been filed with the Intellectual Property Administration Department of the State Council within two years from the date on which it was first commercially exploited anywhere in the world, shall no longer be registered by the Intellectual Property Administration Department of the State Council.

268. Where, after preliminary examination of an application for registration of layout-design, it is found that there is no cause for rejection of the application, the Intellectual Property Administration Department of the State Council shall register it, issue the registration certificate, and announce it.

269. Where the applicant for layout-design registration is not satisfied with the decision of the Intellectual Property Administration Department of the State Council rejecting its or his or her application for registration, it or he or she may, within three months of the date of receipt of the notification, request that the Intellectual Property Administration Department of the State Council make a re-examination. The Intellectual Property Administration Department of the State Council shall, after re-examination, make a decision and notify the applicant for layout-design registration. Where the applicant for layout-design registration is still not satisfied with the decision of re-examination of the Intellectual Property Administration Department of the State Council, it or he or she may, within three months of the date of receipt of the notification, bring a lawsuit before the People's Court.

270. Where, after the registration of a layout-design, the Intellectual Property Administration Department of the State Council finds that the registration does not comply with the provisions of these Regulations; it shall revoke the registration, notify the holder of the right of layout-design, and announce it. Where the holder of the right of layout-design is not satisfied with the decision of the Intellectual Property Administration Department of the State Council revoking the registration of layout-design, it or he or she may, within three months of receipt of the notification, bring a lawsuit before the People's Court.

§5. Ownership and Transfer (Assignment: Licenses)

271. The exclusive right of layout-design is acquired after its being registered with the Intellectual Property Administration Department of the State Council. Any unregistered layout-design shall not be protected under these Regulations.

272. The exclusive right of layout-design shall belong to its creator, except as otherwise prescribed in these Regulations.

273. Where a layout-design is created according to the will and under the charge of a legal person or other organization, which shall bear responsibility for such layout-design, that legal person or other organization shall be the creator. Where a layout-design is created by a natural person, that person shall be the creator.

274. Where a layout-design is created jointly by two or more natural persons, legal persons, or other organizations, the ownership of the exclusive right shall be agreed upon by the joint creators; in the absence of such an agreement or where the agreement is not clear, the exclusive right shall be owned jointly by the creators.

275. Where a layout-design is created in execution of a commission, the ownership of the exclusive right shall be agreed upon by the person having commissioned and the person being commissioned; in the absence of such an agreement or where the agreement is not clear, the exclusive right shall be owned by the person being commissioned.

276. The holder of the right of layout-design may assign its or his or her exclusive right or give other persons a license to exploit its or his or her layout-design.

277. Where the exclusive right of layout-design is assigned, the parties concerned shall prepare a written contract and register it with the Intellectual Property Administration Department of the State Council. The Intellectual Property Administration Department of the State Council shall announce the registration. The assignment of the exclusive right of layout-design shall take effect as of the date of registration.

278. Where a license to exploit a layout-design is given to others, the parties shall prepare a written contract.

§6. Scope of Exclusive Rights

279. The holder of the right of layout-design shall enjoy the following exclusive rights:

(a) reproducing a protected layout-design in its entirety or any part thereof that complies with the requirement of originality; and
(b) commercially exploiting a protected layout-design, an integrated circuit incorporating a protected layout-design, or an article incorporating such an integrated circuit.

§7. LIMITATIONS OF THE SCOPE OF PROTECTION

I. Exemptions

280. Any of the following acts may be performed without the authorization of the holder of the right of layout-design and without any payment of remuneration:

(a) reproducing a protected layout-design for private purposes or for the sole purpose of evaluation, analysis, research, or teaching;
(b) creating a layout-design with originality on the basis of the evaluation or analysis of a protected layout-design referred to in the preceding sub-paragraph; and
(c) reproducing or commercially exploiting a layout-design that is identical with the layout-design of another person but is created independently by oneself.

281. Where a protected layout-design, an integrated circuit incorporating such a layout-design, or an article incorporating such an integrated circuit has been put on the market by, or with the consent of, the holder of the right of layout-design, anyone may exploit it for commercial purposes without the authorization of, nor payment of remuneration to, the holder of the right of layout-design.

II. Non-voluntary Licensing

282. In the case of a national emergency, or in any extraordinary state of affairs, or for the purposes of public interests, or where it is determined according to the law by the People's Court or the Supervision and Inspection Department Against Unfair Competition that there is unfair competition on the part of the holder of the right of layout-design and there is a need to give remedy, the Intellectual Property Administration Department of the State Council may grant a non-voluntary license to exploit the layout-design.

283. The holder of the right of layout-design shall be promptly notified of any decision made by the Intellectual Property Administration Department of the State Council granting a non-voluntary license to exploit a layout-design.

284. In the decision granting a non-voluntary license to exploit a layout-design, the scope and duration of the exploitation shall be specified on the basis of the reasons justifying the grant. The scope shall be limited to non-commercial use for public purposes, or to remedy an act of the holder of the right of layout-design determined, according to the law by the People's Court or the Supervision and Inspection Department Against Unfair Competition, to be one of unfair competition.

285. When the circumstances that led to such non-voluntary license cease to exist and are unlikely to recur, the Intellectual Property Administration Department of the State Council shall, after reviewing upon the request of the holder of the right of layout-design, make a decision to terminate the non-voluntary license.

§8. Duration of Protection

286. The term of protection of the exclusive right of layout-design shall be ten years as of the date of filing an application for registration or from the date on which it was first commercially exploited anywhere in the world, whichever expires earlier. However, no matter whether it has been registered or commercially exploited, a layout-design shall no longer be protected under these Regulations fifteen years after the date of the completion of its creation.

§9. Infringement and Remedies

I. Dispute Resolutions

287. Where a dispute arises as a result of the exploitation of a layout-design without the authorization of the holder of the right of layout-design – that is, the infringement of the exclusive right of layout-design – it shall be settled through consultation by the parties concerned. Where the parties are not willing to consult with each other or where the consultation fails, the holder of the right of layout-design or any interested party may bring a lawsuit before the People's Court or request that the Intellectual Property Administration Department of the State Council handle the matter.

288. When the Intellectual Property Administration Department of the State Council handling the matter considers that the infringement is established, it may order the infringer to stop the infringing act immediately and confiscate or destroy the infringing products or articles. If the party concerned is not satisfied with the decision, he or she may, within fifteen days of date of receipt of the notification, bring a lawsuit before the People's Court in accordance with the Administrative Procedure Law of the People's Republic of China. If, within the said time limit, the infringer does not institute legal proceedings and refuses to stop the infringing act, the Intellectual Property Administration Department of the State Council may apply to the People's Court for compulsory enforcement.

289. The Intellectual Property Administration Department of the State Council may, upon the request of the parties, mediate in the amount of compensation for the damage caused by the infringement of the exclusive right of layout-design. If the mediation fails, the parties may bring a lawsuit before the People's Court in accordance with the Civil Procedure Law of the People's Republic of China.

II. Infringements

290. Except as otherwise prescribed in these Regulations, where any person commits any of the following acts without the authorization of the holder of the right of layout-design, he, she, or it must stop the act immediately and bear liability to compensate for the damage:

(a) reproducing a protected layout-design in its entirety or any part thereof that complies with the requirement of originality; or
(b) importing, selling, or otherwise distributing for commercial purposes a protected layout-design, an integrated circuit incorporating such a layout-design, or an article incorporating such an integrated circuit.

III. Innocent Infringements

291. Where any person commercially exploits an integrated circuit that is incorporated an unlawfully reproduced layout-design, or an article that is incorporated into an integrated circuit with unlawfully reproduced layout-design, and if at the time of acquiring the said integrated circuit or article, that person did not know and had no reasonable grounds to know that the said integrated circuit incorporated an unlawfully reproduced layout-design or the said article incorporated an integrated circuit with unlawfully reproduced layout-design, the commercial exploitation of such integrated circuit or article by that person shall not be deemed as infringing the right of layout-design.

292. After being notified that the integrated circuit or the article is incorporated with an unlawfully reproduced layout-design, the person referred to in the preceding paragraph may, subject to payment of reasonable remuneration to the holder of the right of layout-design, continue to commercially exploit the stock on hand or ordered before the notification.

IV. Damages

293. The amount of compensation for the damage caused by an infringement of the exclusive right of layout-design shall be the profits that the infringer has earned through the infringement or the losses suffered by the person whose right was infringed, including the reasonable expenses paid by the infringed person for the purposes of stopping the infringement.

V. Provisional Measures

294. Where any holder of the right of layout-design or interested party has evidence to prove that another person is infringing or will soon infringe its or his or her exclusive right and has evidence that if such infringing act is not checked or prevented from occurring in time, it is likely to cause irreparable harm to its or his or her 'legitimate' rights, it or he or she may, before any legal proceedings are instituted, request the People's Court to adopt measures for ordering the suspension of relevant acts and the preservation of property.

§10. Overlap and Relation to Other Intellectual Property Laws

295. In addition to this sui generis system, those layout-designs of integrated circuits that are qualified for patentability may, in rare cases, be protected under the patent system.

Chapter 9. Trade Secrets/Confidential Information

§1. Sources: Legislation

296. The Law Against Unfair Competition was adopted at the Third Session of the Standing Committee of the Eighth National People's Congress on 2 September 1993, and became effective 1 December 1993. This Law is expected to be revised soon by the National People's Congress.

297. The 2007 Supreme People's Court's Judicial Interpretations on Unfair Competition provide important judicial guidelines on the trial of unfair competition cases.

298. Infringements against trade secrets are one of the categories of unfair competition regulated by this Law.

§2. The Protection of Trade Secrets/Confidential Information

I. Subject Matter

299. A 'trade secret' refers to technical information and operational information that are not known to the public, are capable of bringing economic benefits to the owner of rights, have practical applicability, and are kept secret by the measure taken by the owner.

300. The Supreme People's Court's Judicial Interpretations on Unfair Competition 2007 provides a detailed explanation of three elements of a trade secret, including:

(a) listing examples of information that may constitute trade secrets, such as client lists;
(b) providing that, regarding the term 'not known to the public', information must not be easily obtained by the people who would usually handle information of that kind; and
(c) providing that the measures that an owner of the information are required to take to maintain its confidentiality must be reasonable, specific, and effective.

II. Scope of Protection

301. An operator may not adopt the following means to infringe the trade secret of another person:

(a) obtaining the trade secret of another person by stealing, promising gain, resorting to coercion, or other improper means;

(b) disclosing, using, or allowing others to use the trade secret of another person obtained by the means mentioned in the preceding item;
(c) disclosing, using, or allowing others to use the trade secret that he or she has obtained by breaking an engagement or disregarding the requirement of the owner of the trade secret to maintain the secret in confidence; or
(d) obtaining, using, or disclosing the trade secret of another person when he or she knows or should have known the illegal acts mentioned in the preceding items.

III. Liabilities and Remedies

302. Where any party infringes the trade secret of another person, the Administration of Industry and Commerce shall order the infringer to desist from the illegal act and may, according to circumstances, impose on him or her, a fine of more than CNY 10,000 and less than CNY 200,000. Where the infringement constitutes a crime, he or she shall, in accordance with the Criminal Law, be prosecuted for his or her criminal liability.

Chapter 10. Geographical Indications and Appellations of Origin

303. In accordance with the Trademark Law 2015, a geographical indication identifies the goods as originating from the territory where a given quality, reputation, or other characteristic of the goods is essentially attributable to the natural or humane elements of that territory. Geographical indications are included in geographical names, but not all geographical names are qualified to be geographical indications.

304. A geographical indication may be registered as a collective mark or certificate mark to the extent that it is qualified for the requirements of such two categories of marks. A trademark containing the geographical indication with respect to goods not originating in the territory indicated so as to mislead the public shall not be registered or used.

305. Besides a trademark legal system, an interested party of a geographical indication may also rely on a Chinese unfair competition legal system to fight against the acts.

Selected Bibliography

Books

Zheng, Chengsi, *Intellectual Property Enforcement in China: Leading Cases and Commentary*. Hong Kong: Sweet & Maxwell, (English).

Xue, H. & Zheng, Chengsi, *Chinese Intellectual Property Law in the 21st Century*. Hong Kong: Sweet & Maxwell, (English).

Xue, H., *Intellectual Property in the Network Age*. Beijing: Law Press of China, 2000.

Xue, H., *Intellectual Property in Electronic Commerce*. Beijing: Law Press of China, 2004.

Xue, H., International Intellectual Property Law @ Crossroad, Beijing: Law Press of China, 2012.

Journals

China Intellectual Property News (Chinese).

China Law Report (Chinese, only partially translated into English).

China Patent News (Chinese).

China Patents & Trademarks (Chinese and English).

China Trademark (Chinese).

Copyright (China) (Chinese).

Copyright bulletin (UNESCO) (English and other languages, including Chinese).

European Intellectual Property Review (English).

Electronics Intellectual Property (Chinese).

GRUR International (Max Planck Institute) (German).

Intellectual Property Studies (Chinese Academy of Social Sciences) (Chinese and English).

International Review of Industrial Property and Copyright Law (I.I.C.) (Max Planck Institute) (English).

Journal of Intellectual Property (Chinese).

World Intellectual Property Report (English).

World Licensing Law Report (English).

Selected Bibliography

Index

The numbers here refer to paragraph numbers.

Index

www.ingramcontent.com/pod-product-compliance
Lightning Source LLC
Chambersburg PA
CBHW071355230926
51846CB00002B/562
9789041162472